Acknowledgements

I would like to thank the entire Loyola High School community for all of their support and encouragement in writing this book. The Greatest Google Generation has been a passion of mine for many years. World War II is a time period that has captivated us all. The era and events have inspired me to teach others about the sacrifices made by previous generations so that we can inspire and teach future generations to come.

Levi Line
Social Science Instructor
Loyola High School 2012
lline@loyolahs.edu

Special Thanks:

To my Loving wife and best friend: Danielle Line

To both my Grandfathers: Bill Line and Bill Koznar

To the Greatest Generation: Thank you for the sacrifices your generation made to allow for future generations to live free!!

THE GREATEST

Google

GENERATION

As of September 30th, 2011, there are roughly 2,889,000 WWII veterans alive in the USA according to the U.S. Department of Veteran Affairs. Worldwide, there are about 5,250,000 still around as of late 2011. "**The Greatest Generation**" is a term coined by journalist Tom Brokaw to describe the generation who grew up in the United States during the deprivation of the Great Depression, and then went on to fight in World War II, as well as those whose productivity within the war's home front made a decisive material contribution to the war effort.

As of September 30th, 1990 there have been roughly 4 million people a year born in the United States alone." **The Google Generation**" is a common name in the US and other Western nations for the group of people born from the early or mid 1990s to the present. The generation has grown up with the World Wide Web, which became increasingly available from 1991 onwards. The Google youth are highly connected, as many of this generation have had lifelong use of communications and media technologies such as the World Wide Web, instant messaging, text messaging, MP3 players, mobile phones and smartphone technologies.

INTRODUCTION

Most if not all surviving members of the Greatest Generation couldn't tell you how to work an IPad or how to text message. Most of the Google Youth could not tell you about the sacrifices that were made by the Greatest Generation to allow for future generations to enjoy such technological splendors. To a Google Youth events like, "D-Day", "Bastogne", "Guadalcanal", "Iwo Jima" and the "Battle for Berlin" can only be found in their video games. It is crucial that our Google Youth understand the sacrifices that were made by the Greatest Generation so that they can teach future generations to come. Mr. Lines class embarked on a journey that allowed for the Google student to meet and interact with surviving members of the Greatest Generation. With around 1,000 veterans dying each day the chance to meet and come face to face with one was rare.

Mr. Lines class interviewed over one hundred veterans and civilians who lived during World II. All of the veterans who took part in the project played major contributions to the war effort. The "Greatest Google Generation", project allowed the students to come face to face with surviving members of World War II. Students heard first hand accounts of how the Greatest Generation lived and survived during the Great Depression and World War II. Student interviewed surviving members from the Pacific and European campaigns and also had civilians describe how life was like for them on the American home front. Being able to hear first hand accounts from people who lived during those challenging times can never be duplicated in any movie or video game. The students were able to listen and appreciate all that the Greatest Generation did for them and future generations to come. From acts of heroism on the battlefield to acts of sacrifice at home, the Google Generation can now truly appreciate all that was done for them and for future generations to come. When the Google Generation looks back at this project and the Greatest Generation has moved on, one will be able to explain with pride that they had the honor to meet and interview a member from the **"Greatest Generation."**

Teacher: Mr. Levi Line
Veteran/ Civilian Interviewed: Bill Line
Relationship to the teacher: Grandfather
Date and location of the interview: September of 2003. Euless TX

My Grandfather introduced me to the War when I was a young boy. I could remember sitting on his lap watching old World War II movies and him explaining his experiences in the war. I never truly appreciated what he told me until I studied it in college. Realizing I wanted to teach the youth of the nation the history of the war, I made every attempt to pick his brain before it was too late. The knowledge I gained from the years we spent together will last me a life time and will be passed down through our family for future generations to come.

Q- What were you doing before you joined the military?

A- I was a bare knuckles boxer and auto mechanic before the war

Q- Where were you living?

A- I was living in Euless Texas

Q- Were you attending school?

A- I had just graduated and was trying to make a career from either boxing or working in an auto shop.

Q- Did you have a sweetheart?

A- No I did not

Q- Where did you go during the war?

A- After we were attacked at Pearl Harbor I felt duty bound to enlist with my other friends at the local recruitment station. I enlisted in the Army and trained at Fort Sill Oklahoma to become a Military Mechanic.

Q- Where were you stationed first?

A- I was first sent to Melbourne Australia to receive extra training and to receive my assignment for the war. After being assigned to Douglas MacArthur and his wife to repair any problem that went wrong with their vehicles. From Australia I was stationed on the Philippines along side McArthur. His wife stayed behind in Australia.

Q- How did it feel to be assigned to General Douglas McArthur?

A- I really didn't realize how important he was until I spent time with him and understood the role he played. I took allot from him and our experience. When we had to flee the islands I saw the determination in his face and understood his commitment to this war.

Q- What was your general attitude towards the war?

A- I truly felt that the United States was involved in a larger than life conflict against other nations who wanted to control other peoples. I joined out of my love for this country.

Q- I understood that if it wasn't for the Pacific Campaign I would not be here today, could you explain why?

A- Well, after the Marine Corps and the Army fled the Philippines, I went back to Melbourne and there I met your grandmother. We were both young and very much in love. I was an old country boy from Texas and she was a beautiful Aussie who didn't give me the time of day, but after much persistence I won her heart.

Q- What was your most memorable experience in the war?

A- My most memorable experience in the war was meeting your grandmother. I didn't witness to much action in the war because we were usually away from the front lines. But I will always remember the first time I laid eyes on your Grandmother.

Q- What have you taken from this war that has made you a better person?

A- The war has really taught me the importance of freedom and what it takes to remain free. I can remember those back home who sacrificed so much to keep this nation safe. Our generation didn't think twice about going to war, it was just something that we did.

Student: Michael Willoughby

Where were you during World War 2?

"I was born on the island of Cebu and later I moved Manilla as a young teen. I stayed in Manila during the majority of World War two and I also remember the battle of Manila in (doesn't remember date)

What do you remember about the Battle of Manila?

I remember the invasion of the Japanese and the extensive fighting. Luckily I ran away with a group of my friends to the hills. I remember hiding in the mountains and hearing babies cry.

And how old were you at this time?

16 years old. I remember, it was two years before I met Benard (husband)

How scared were you in those caves?

"Boy, you don't even know what scared is. The cave was real damp and really cramped. We were too scared to leave in fear we would get spotted. I remember one of my friends left the cave and she never came back. (crying)"

How did you know when it was safe to leave?

American troops found our cave after the 4th day. I don't know how we survived but we just did.

Were you relocated? I know the battle lasted for a month in Manila.

Yes we were relocated to an outskirt city protected by the United States. After the war ended, it was there that I fell in love with Bernard.

What were you doing at the time of the war?

I was working at a Mini mart in Manila. I was still in high school but my job was a cash register.

Do you remember any fighting before the invasion of Manila?

"No I don't, you know I have somewhat a bad memory."

Do you remember much about Bernard? What division he was a part of?

"No I can't remember. It was so long ago and I just forgot these things"

I remember a couple days ago we talked about the caves, do you remember how many people were with you?

"It was me, three of my friends (girls) and about 5 older guys. There was this family with a newborn baby that I could never forget because he would never shut up. Haha."

Rashaad Washington

Joynne Valien

Grandmother

4/24/12 at her grandsons house

       I chose my grandma for this interview because she is the only relative in America who

has lived through the WWII time period. Not only that, she is a very interesting person. She was

the oldest out of her brothers and sisters and now she is the only one left from them. I view my

grandma as one huge history book and an inspiring role model. These are the reasons for why

I decided to do the interview on my grandmother even though she wasn't part of the army.

9. What was your everyday life like? I was very active... I was a teenager. I regretted not being a

delivery worker to be part of the war. But at my current age I was too young to understand the

impact of the war.

How did your friends feel about the war? Everybody in my class was ready to fight; they had a deep hatred towards \

the Germans. Patriotism was practiced at school singing songs and all. We had to sacrifice food and more for the

war.

10. What did you do to pass the time? I worked at recreational parks, coach, supervise, and workout. But my father

and brother worked in a shipyard.

2. Do you remember how you felt about Japan bombing Pearl Harbor? When I heard about this, I wished I really

was a boy. I was ready to go to war. I lost a lot of friends because of that Japanese sneak attack.

3. Did you enlist or were you drafted? I wanted to enlist with the navy. I used to wear my sailor hats to impersonate

them, but for women to be part of the navy we had to either be a secretary or nurse which I wasn't trying to do.

(laughter)

Ross Steinbach

World War II Civilian Interview: Bob Sellars

-Step Grandfather

-Telephone

How old were you when the war started?

-Born in 1932,

-In the middle of the War (Japan and Europe)

-Both Going on in 1942- 10 years old

Did you see any changes in your daily life during the war?

-"No, my life did not change very much because of the war."

-People who had cars had stickers on their cars dictating how much gas they could buy. Sometimes they had to take the bus because simply that they did have enough gas to waste going somewhere.

-At night there were air raid drills.

Did your parents have jobs that changed because of the war?

- His father was a head chemist at a tire factory. The factory stopped making tires for regular cars and started making tires for military vehicles.

Do you remember Pearl Harbor?

-3:30 on a Sunday afternoon.

- At his grandmothers house in Philadelphia.

-Aunt came down the stair saying that news came over the radio that Pearl Harbor had be attacked by the Japanese.

- Made sure that they got back on the bus to home because the busses would stop running.

-People on the east coast were not afraid of the Japanese attacking.

-They were much more afraid of the Germans.

-People that lived on the coast could see smoke from German torpedo's that were shot at freight ships going to Europe.

Story about his Cousin who was in the European campaign:

-Cousin came back from 3 or 4 years of combat.

-He was an artillery officer.

-During his time there he collected things off dead German officers.

-He collected things like helmets, ammunition, rifles, and side arms.

-He packed all the stuff he collected into boxes used to store artery rounds and about a year after the war ended they finally came back to the states.

-His Cousin did not know whether or not he would get them or not.

-Here is a picture of Mr. Sellars wearing a German helmet that his cousin gave to him when the packages arrived.

Student: Ian Ross

Veteran/Civilian: Charles Ross

Relationship to the student: Grandfather

Date and location of interview: At my house with my father.

I choose to interview my dad about my grandfather for a few reasons. One was because I didn't know a lot about my grandfather because he died when I was five. Another was that I knew he was a cook so I wanted to know about non-combat troops in the war.

What were you doing before you joined the military?

I was going to high school and work odd jobs. I was actually applying for my citizenship at the time and they said I could get it by joining the armed forces.

Where were you living?

I was living in a suburb outside Detroit after I emigrated from Scotland.

Did you have a sweetheart?

I didn't have a sweetheart but I married the love of my life when I got out of the military.

Did you enlist or were you drafted?

I was offered a quicker way of getting my citizenship and I viewed it as a chance to serve my future home country.

What did you envision it would be like after you joined?

I wanted to be a cook because I had experience in the kitchen and I felt that was a good way to help the troops without having to kill someone.

What do you remember about your first days in the military?

I remember doing basic training and getting assigned to the Pacific fleet as a cook.

What were you doing during the war?

I was stationed on a couple different battleships and aircraft carriers in the Pacific. I would wake up everyday and make hundreds of scrambled eggs and bacon for all the troops. My everyday experiences ranged from cooking to organizing storerooms within the ships. My living conditions were separate from the barracks of the other sailors so they were a step up.

What was it like after the war?

I got home and I worked on a golf course and started a family with my new wife.

What did you do? How did your career develop after that?

After that I became a salesman for large tractors and machinery, and I eventually went on to own several golf courses.

Student: Randy Suh
Veteran: Clifton H. Clarkson
Relationship to student: fellow parishioner
Date and location of the interview: 4/21/12

       I have chosen Clifton H. Clarkson for the interview because not only was he a fellow parishioner and lived close to me; but also, he lived a very different life in the military that no one really thinks of. When people are asked to think about the life soldiers, they normally think of soldiers living on the frontline and getting shot at. In Clifton Clarkson's case, he lived through the other side of the life as a soldier, just as many others have. He was very intellectual and strong. He served as an engineer and an architect that was part of an infantry unit.

Questions and Answers

Q: What were you doing before you joined the military?
A: I was a student at St. Bernice High school

Q: Where did you live?
A: St. Bernice, Indiana

Q: Where did you go to join?
A: Terre Haute, Indiana

Q: Did you enlist or were you drafted? If enlisted, what motivated you to enlist?
A: I enlist because I would have been drafted into the military the moment I turned eighteen.

Q: Did any friends enlist with you?
A: Yes, but not at the same time. They enlisted a bit later into the military. I was the first among my high school friends.

Q: Why did you choose your branch of service?
A: It gave me a chance to go to engineering school.

Q: What did you envision it would be like after you joined?
A: I envisioned that the military life would be something I would be interested in because I had heard a lot about the discipline that was involved and I liked discipline because even though I was bit of a renegade, it was something I needed. The education that was promised for me was very good for me too. I also liked the idea that there would be some sort of a control book in my life.

Q: What do you remember about you first days in the military?
A: It was miserable, only because I had to take a number of exams.

Q: Do you remember anything about your instructors?
A: I remember all my instructors, especially a corporal named Corporal Birdy from basic training. He was as nasty as anyone can imagine. The corporal was supposedly "doing his job" and he was good at it too. I think my friends and I came close to hating him

Q: What were you doing during the war?
A: For most of the war, I was still living at home, attending school, and living my teenage life. I had couple of odd jobs. I did what most teenagers did play sports and hang out with friends. St. Bernice was more of a suburb than a city, like a bedroom community. It was an easy and carefree life. Besides having to life up to certain standards, we had almost no limit to our freedom. I joined the army on June 26, 1946, just before the war ended. I was part of the 88th infantry in Italy at the free territory of Trieste. I was at Trieste on an occupation duty, but my real assignment was a classified engineering position.

Q: What was your everyday life like?
A: The military life during basic training was not easy because the work and learning were hard and difficult. When he was on occupation duty at the free territory, my life was easy. I had a class A uniforms every day, and enough food to eat. The work was more intellectually demanding rather than physically.

Q: Did you write many letters home? Did people write to you?
A: My mother wrote to me regularly. At the time when I was over at Trieste, he wanted to get married, but I was not at the age where the military would allow me to get married; therefore, I wrote a threatening letter home saying that I will not come home until my parents allowed me to get married.

Q: What was the food like? Did you always have enough food?
A: I always had enough supply of food. One time when he was at the mess hall in camp Atterbury, Indiana, I was really hungry because at my age, at the time, I had a big appetite. So I got a lot of food on the silver tray and sat down next to two sergeants. The sergeants on purposely talked about horrific stories, which caused me to lose my appetite.

Video for interview: http://youtu.be/KGcuHV4-Ryo

Student: Daniel Paton

My grandfather, Bob Pernecky, grew up in Chicago. The war started when he was around 13 or 14 years old, and he always wanted to join the army, but he just wasn't old enough. I asked him questions about life as a civilian during the war and the effects it had on the community.

1. What was your personal reaction to the Peal Harbor attack?

"The whole nation was very surprised, as was. All of the people were thinking, excuse my language, kill the dam Japs. The people were very upset at what happened and fully supported the war. I was to young to join the war at the time but I wanted to get in as soon as I turned 18."

2. What was the general attitude of your community towards the war? (Chicago)

"The community population was 110% behind war. The sacrifices that the average household had to make were very great. Men left wives and families to support the war, and many of the wives were forced to get high-working jobs. I remember there were orange and blue stamps for certain types of products you could get. One was better than the other. One product I especially remember is Soap, all the nice soap went to the army, so we had no good soap left at home. The substitute for this soap was 'oaky dope.' The saying 'Rosy the Riveter' became synonymous with women who worked with aircraft, steel, and other industries."

3. How did the media portray the war?

"The radio, press, newspaper...they were all in full support of the war and being the 'G.I. Joe' figure. America acknowledged the accolades given to our armed forces. People who went to join the war were completely naïve to the horrors the war actually encountered."

4. Were there any other motives to join war besides for patriotism?

"There were many reasons that all the boys on my block that were a little bit older than me went to join the war. Another common motive for joining the war would be to get a job. Many of the older kids couldn't find any jobs because economy conditions were poor so they thought, 'why not go to the army where we get food and pay?' I remember a joke that says,' In the army, you get paid 21$ a day, once a month."

5. What were economical conditions like in your neighborhood?

"In Chicago we were greatly affected by the war. Of course everybody was on the train for the war, but eventually people started to resent it due to its breakdown of the economy, not to mention the thousands of dead soldiers."

Student: Anthony Parada
Civilian Interviewed: Don Haslwanter
Relationship to Student: Grandfather
Date & Location of Interview: April 18, 2012, Haslwanter Residence, Pasadena, California.

I chose to interview my grandpa because I knew that he lived during the time of World War II, and I wanted to find out what he remembered from the time. I was not entirely sure if he fought in the war or not, but I was curious to find out. I ended up discovering that he didn't take part in the war because he was only about 10, but he still remembered some interesting events that occurred. Until the interview I had never sat down with my grandpa and talked with him about the war and was glad I received the opportunity to do it.

Q: Do you remember how you felt about Japan or the war in Europe prior to Pearl Harbor? Do you remember the day Pearl Harbor was attacked?
A: I remember when Pearl Harbor happened, but at the time I wasn't quite aware of the situation. I knew that Japan had been trying to take over China and had sided with the European powers of Germany and Italy to take over that part of the world.

Q: What was your everyday life like? Did you always have enough food? How were your other supplies and equipment?
A: We had food, but we also had food and gasoline rationing. If you had an *A* sticker you were entitled to buy 10 gallons of gas a week. If you worked for the government or the war effort and had to travel, you got more gas to use. And then meat and sugar were rationed during a time where women had to be friendly with their butchers in order to get the best cuts of meat. We never went hungry though. It's just that some much of the food was going towards the war effort.

Q: What did you do to pass the time? Did you ever keep a journal or diary?
A: No. I usually just read the newspaper and listened to the radio for news as far as the war was concerned because you're looking at a time prior to television.

Q: Do you remember V-E Day and V-J Day when the war ended? How did you celebrate? What did the end of the war mean to you?
A: Yes I do. There was just a large celebration at school. I was too young to get drunk. After the war like became a little more slow-paced. During the war my father worked a daytime job and at night he worked at a machine shop where he helped build parts for the P-38 aircraft. After the war the aircrafts were no longer needed, so my dad only had to work one job and we got to see him more.

Q: What was life like after the war? Where were you living? What work did you do?
A: Well, of course, I was still in school. But I sold magazines and newspapers. That's about all I did.

Extra Discussion:
I remember one time where the Japanese launched a two-man sub off the coast of here and were trying to hit some oil and gas storage tanks. They didn't hit anything, but it was interesting that things got to that stage. I remember blackouts happened. People covered buildings with painted canvases in order to camouflage them from enemy aircraft. They also set up cables in Long Beach that ran across the air. These cables' use was to get stuck in enemy aircrafts' propellers. On these hills some anti-aircraft guns were set up as well, but they were never actually fired. Also, for possible air raids all the homeowners had to have blackout shades, which covered the windows and didn't

let any of the light shine out. In fact, my dad built a thing where you'd pull the shade down. If everything was dark, enemy aircraft couldn't see what was below. The street lamps were also turned off and an air raid captain was posted on several blocks in case any situation was to happen. Army jeeps were used to get around, and they had a tiny light attached to them so they could see about 5 to 10 feet in front of them. I remember standing on a building and seeing how long it took for the lights to go out because the lights weren't hooked up to computers. Their switches had to be turned manually. I would wait for about 5 to 10 minutes before all the streetlights went out. Each blackout lasted for about an hour or so but was spread throughout all of Los Angeles. I only remember two blackouts that lasted for any length of time. We had a lot of warnings but they never blacked out the city. I just thought that was exciting because people would try to drive home from work but couldn't turn their headlights on, so it was pretty mass panic at that time.

For the full interview visit http://www.youtube.com/watch?v=Wy7y4UeDQtM

BN: No, I didn't really write letters home because I was single during the early part of being in the military. However, I was on leave when I met my future wife, so when I returned, I began writing a lot of letters to her.

KO: What was the food like over there?

BN: It was actually very good, unless we were out training in the boondocks. But other than that they fed us very well.

KO: What do you remember most about V-E Day and V-J Day when the war ended?

BN: When V-E and V-J Day occurred, I was around 16 years old, so I wasn't old enough to be in the military, but I was excited to hear the news, and I was impressed with the efforts of the troops overseas. I also had older brothers and some family friends that fought in the war that all came home safe, which was always a blessing.

Kyle Otazu
Mr. Bob Neace
Church Friend
4-24-12, Pasadena

I chose to interview Mr. Neace because I knew that he was a war veteran and that he was alive during World War II and experienced the events that transpired during the war. He did not actually fight in the war due to his age, but he had

relatives and friends who did. He did however have two years of experience in the Army after both WWII and the Korean War were over.

KO: What were you doing before you joined the military? Were you attending school?

BN: I was living in California at this time, and I was studying at the Pasadena Nazarene College, and then from there I went to USC and got a Master's in Psychiatric Sciences.

KO: Do you remember how you felt about either Japan or the war in Europe prior to Pearl Harbor?

BN: In 1941, when the attacks occurred, I was around 11 years old, so I wasn't as politically aware of the events of the war, but as with many Americans, I had a very strong dislike towards the Japanese after the bombing of Pearl Harbor.

KO: What do you remember about your first days in the military? What was the branch of service that you joined?

BN: I went into the Army after I got my Master's degree from USC. At first, I went in to get my officer's commission, but before I received it I was inducted into boot camp. From there I became a private, and then I became a 2nd lieutenant. I spent two years in the Army, and I worked with Mental Hygiene, which was where I helped with people who were stressed or homesick, etc.

KO: Do you remember anything about your instructors?

BN: I don't remember them with much fondness; they were tough and trained us hard, which I was OK with, I had expected that. But I think they went overboard in terms of their being too harsh to the cadets that were training.

KO: So I understand that you weren't in the military at the time of WWII? Where did you go when you were in the Army?

BN: I was first stationed at Fort Ord on Monterey, California. After that I went to San Antonio, and then to Fort Knox in Kentucky. That took up my first year in the Army, and then the second year I spent entirely at Fort Ord.

KO: What was your everyday life like? Did you write letters home?

Student: Nathan Hadley (Period 5)
Civilian Interviewed: Luis Brito
Relationship to the student: Grandfather
Date and location of the interview: Grandpa's house in Los Angeles, California

I chose to interview my grandpa because I knew he was someone that could recall times and events that happened during the time and also because it was easy for me to interview him because I didn't really have to travel. My grandpa was around 17 at the time.

Q: What was your everyday life like?
A: My everyday life was to go to school everyday, have fun on the weekends, and play soccer as much as I could. Also, I since I was almost done with school, I was thinking about working with my dad who was good at fixing things.

Q: When you first heard the war had started, what was your reaction and everybody else's reaction?
A: When I first heard of it, I didn't really care for it too much being in El Salvador and many of us Latinos didn't do much during the time. The only thing I cared about was if someone tried to bomb us so I prayed every night from then on I still do it till this day. But, for some reason my dad was interested by German radio and he knew how much more World War II meant for them compared to us.

Q: Did you know anybody that fought in World War II?
A: I didn't know anybody who fought until I came to America. That is when I met some people that did and they told me about there experiences during the war. I felt bad at times when they told me stories about how many friends they had lost during the war because I could remember that I didn't really care for it when I was younger.

Q: What was it like after the war?
A: After the war, in El Salvador, there was really too much of a difference except for the fact that some people like me knew that there was no way that we could get into the war. Also, for people like my mom who got emotional a lot of the time were happy because they knew that many people weren't doing now and dying in a way that was not peaceful.

Q: When you came to America and asked people about their reactions from the war, what were they?
A: I first came to America around 1950 so that was like 5 years ago that it ended. At first, I really couldn't ask many people about there experiences because at that time, there were still many racists and segregation was still going on. But after they had stopped that, many people said that war was a lot different than what they pictured it as because they knew they would be fighting for their country but they didn't know about the issues they would have psychologically because either they had friends that died, arms or legs that were gone, or having bad nightmares. But all in all, they still said it was worth fighting for.

Student: Nick Moscicki
Civilian interviewed: Elena Catherine Moscicki
Relationship to me: Grandmother
4-22-12 Los Angeles, CA

I chose to interview my grandmother Elena because she is an Italian- American who was a teenager during World War II and whose father was in the United States Army during the War. I wanted to see her point of view as a civilian during the war and also as a child of someone who served our country during this war.

Q1: How old were you and where were you when Pearl Harbor happened?
I was nine years old when Pearl Harbor happened and we were living in the suburbs of Los Angeles. When I heard about it was in the morning and my father was the one who told us about it.

Q2: When and why did your father enlist in the military?
My father enlisted in the military immediately after Pearl Harbor the war around 1942 and he enlisted because he wanted joined the military for no other reason than to fight and help his country.

Q3: What were your feelings towards his decision on joining the military?
Nana (my great-grandmother) and I were not very happy that he joined the military but we had really no say in it because he would always do what he wanted to do.

Q4: Was life at home different after he left to the war?
Well, Nana and I were not able to do some of the things we wanted to do. Your great-grandfather did not want Nana driving while he was gone at war and because of this we had to walk to many places or find someone else to take us. Also we had to use food stamps to buy food. If we wanted sugar or something we would have to use food stamps to buy them.

Q5: Where was your father stationed during the war?
My father actually never went to Europe but instead he was stationed in Missouri because he helped with the building of tanks and jeeps going over to Europe.

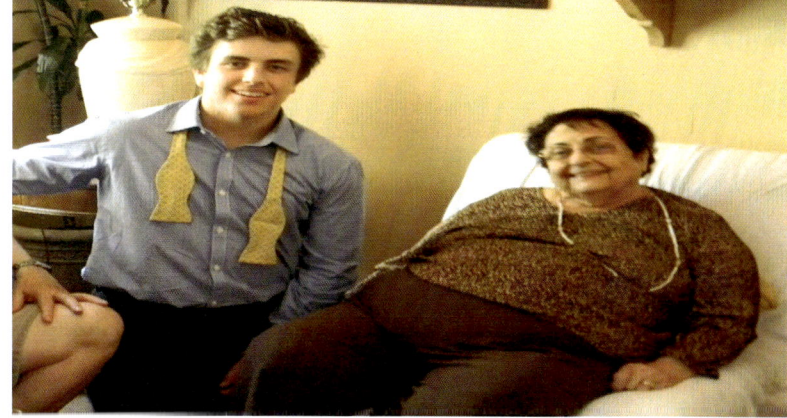

Dakota Low
Rosemary Low
Grandmother
April 24th, 2012 6:17pm

I chose to interview my grandmother for this interview because she has such a great knowledge of World War Two. My Grandmother has met and known many decorated officers and spies for the United States of America. She is 68 years old, and was born during WWII.

Q: Where were you living during the war?
A: Well I was born in 1943; My parents didn't want me born in camp. So my mother hand wrote a letter to President Roosevelt asking if they could be let out of camp stating all of their reasons. So the President granted them the right to be let out of camp as long as they didn't go to any of the coasts. So we ended up in Denver, Colorado.
Q: Do you know any War heroes?
A: Well not war heroes but I knew a spy for the US. He was full-blooded Japanese and spoke fluent Japanese. So most of the Japanese men went into the 442nd and went to fight in Europe so they would never get mixed up and risk being shot by the wrong people thinking they were Japanese soldiers. But our friend, he went to fight in the Pacific War with Japan and he was in Okinawa and places of that sort, and he pretended that he was a Japanese soldier that was deaf and dumb. He would sneak across, wondering around where the soldiers were and listened to them. Trying to see what their next move would be and because he acted like he was deaf and dumb they never came to the conclusion that he was an American Spy. And when he was sneak across back, his own soldiers would fire him on because they didn't know he was an American.
Q: What did you do when the War ended?
A: Well we moved from Denver into Los Angeles, actually near Loyola. We lived on Arlington and Pico. We rented a house and since everybody had to find jobs and didn't have money, we lived with three or four families in one house. Then after that we moved to East Los Angeles.
Q: Do you remember what everyday life was like in the camp?
A: No, but I've been told many stories. They said that the buildings were single wall constructions, with no insulation. My mother was stationed in Heart Mountain Wyoming, she remembers the nights as very cold. And only having one blanket to keep her warm.
Q: What was everyday like?
A: Well when we first got home from Denver, we didn't have a lot of money so sometimes we wouldn't have a meal because the money we had, we needed to get to work the next day. But other than we would play outside everyday and have fun but only during the summer because we would go to school and then go to work after school.

Student: Evan Lewis
Civilians Interviewed: Ginny Foglia, Stella Frysinger
Relationship to the student: Neighbor
Date and location of the Interview: April 21st, 2012- Ginny and Stella's home

I chose to interview my neighbors because I wanted to know what it was like to be not just a civilian during World War II, but also a kid. I also wanted to know what changes and sacrifices kids had to make during the War. Finally, I wanted to know what it was like to be a part of "The Greatest Generation," and "The Google Generation."

1. Do you remember how you felt about Japan or the war in Europe prior to Pearl Harbor?

I don't remember that not much before the war (Ginny was 10 and Stella was 5). But I remember Pearl Harbor being bombed. I remember the victory gardens where people would grow their own food. I remember us having stamps or rations allowed us to only get certain foods and other items at certain times.

2. What did you do during the war?

Collect all sorts of things like cigarettes, stamps and cans. I also remember going to the movies and seeing news updates about the war in the theaters. I would march in the parades with all the other kids. I remember there being a lot of USO booths recruiting people to join the war effort.

3. What was your everyday life like?

Yes, it was very stressful. Especially when you had a family member or friend fighting. If you lost a friend it was very sad. The war as a part of our everyday lives. My uncle fought in the Philippians, and I remember him telling me he had bugs crawling all over him and he ate so many pineapples that the teeth rotted from the acid. But, everyday life didn't change dramatically. We didn't know what was going on exactly, but we knew it was big because of all the cutbacks and rationing and all of the USO booths. I remember when the boys came hom e, they didn't want to talk about what happened.

4. Do you remember V-E Day and VJ Day when the war ended?

Yes, I was on my way to West Virginia to see my uncle, who fought in the South Pacific, when we heard the war had ended in Europe. There was a lot of jubilation and many exited people. I remember when the bombs were dropped in Hiroshima, Japan and seeing all of the bodies from the Holocaust on the news.

5. What was it like after the war?

Life became very peaceful and there were a lot of jubilant people. I remember friends and family coming home and how happy everyone was to see them. I remember a lot of soldiers getting married right after the war and the soldiers getting jobs and going to college. Many men went to war just so they could get an education and because of the GI Bill.

Student: Mateo Le Noir
Civilian Interviewed: Dalia Martinez
Relationship: Great Grandmother
Date and Location: April 23 2012 in Los Angeles

       I chose my great-grandmother for this project, because she always told me stories about how her life was when she was a child. She also described to me how she had to ration food. Because of that, I was told that I should not waste any food. She was not very wealthy, and her parents did not speak English. This made it harder for her to learn; yet she was still valedictorian at her high school. I was always told about her life, but never about the time of World War II. This is why I wanted to find out.

Q1. How and when did you first find out about the war?
- How did you react?

A1. I was in the school yard when they played over the intercom that the United States
    was in war with Japan.
- I was only thirteen at the time, so it was scary, but because I was so young I was oblivious.

Q2. Did things change in your life when the war started?
- How so?

A2. Things were different, because we had to not only ration food, but we had to use
    things that were like food stamps, except they were not only for food. Whatever we
    did not have stamps for, we could not buy.

Q3. How difficult was it having to use stamps.

A3. It was difficult because we only had a few stamps for a month. People were selling
    their stamps as well.
Q4. Were you for the war or against it?
- Why?

A4. I was against the war.
- I was against it, because I knew people would get killed.

Q5. What was the most challenging part about having to live through the war?

A5. It was not really that bad, I was used to living that way.

http://www.youtube.com/watch?v=q04A5ozfTzl

Kyle Beadles

Robert Kilpatrick

Grandfather

4/23/12

I decided to interview my grandfather because when I was little I remember him telling me stories about his military days. He was enlisted as a pilot during World War II. I knew that he became a flight instructor before he returned home on leave. Also my dad has told me some of the stories that my grandfather went through while in the military. I never have really talked to my grandpa about being in the military so I thought this would be a great project to do on him and learn about his military career.

!.) What were you doing before you joined the military?

A: I was in my third year of college.

2.) Did you enlist or were you drafted?

A: I enlisted because to be honest I knew that I was going to be drafted. I felt that I would be more proud to be in the military if I enlisted instead of being drafted into the military.

3.) What do you remember about your first days in the military?

A: I was sent to Indianapolis, Minnesota on January 15, 1943. Then after being there for a few days I was sent to Wisconsin for my first day of flight training.

4.) What was everyday life like?

A: The first flight training facility was at a former hangar. We were bunked at a school with decent food and we got to meet the local girls. We were there for about a few months, then sent to Iowa for pre flight training. We were sent to a lot of different cities on short notice. This training was to weed out the guys who could not take the physical abilities to be in the military. They had us go through an obstacle course, boxing, football, and basketball. The food was reasonable Navy food.

5.) Did you come home on leave?

A: Yes I came back to my family in February 1944 and road the Old Captian railroad from Chicago to Los Angeles.

6.) What was it like after the war?

A: When I first got out of the military I was given $3,000 in cash, then when I got back in California I went to Chicago Law School, which I really enjoyed.

Graham Good
Interviewed: Dorothy Good
Veteran: Earl Good
Relationship: Grandson
Date/ Location: April 23, 2012 at Nazareth House

I chose to interview my grandmother about my grandfather because I never got to meet my grandfather who died when my father was young. I wanted to get to learn about my grandfather and wanted to see what his life was like before the war, and how his military life and experience played out throughout the war.

Questions and Answers

1. What was Earl doing before he joined the military?

Earl was born in San Diego and was a native of California. He attended University High School in Los Angeles, California. Before the war, he was a draftsman for Lockheed Aircraft Manufacturing Air Company. Unfortunately, the night he returned home to Los Angeles, the war broke out.

2. Do you remember about how you and Earl felt about the war in Europe prior to Pearl Harbor; also, do you remember how you and Earl felt the day Pearl Harbor was bombed?

Earl and I were young and not interested in foreign affairs at the time. When we would see Hitler on the television screen or see the Germans and they're strange signs and walks, we would laugh and think of them as jokes. We weren't really that focused on what was occurring in Europe during the time. However, when Pearl Harbor was bombed, everyone in Los Angeles was quiet and the day was very somber and gloomy. The streets were empty and nobody was in a good mood on that day, and the United States was very dreary after that day.

3. Did Earl enlist in the army and how did he feel when joining the army?

Earl enlisted in the army shortly after the bombing of Pearl Harbor, and went to sign up in Downtown LA. He was very excited about joining the army and really wanted to be an engineer. However, when he arrived to boot camp, he went into the Air Force and became a bomber.

4. What was Earl doing during the war and what jobs or assignments did Earl have throughout it? Also, did he ever share any memorable or scary experiences he has with you?

Earl was a trainer for the cadets at Victorville Army Air Force Base. He would train the cadets on how to be precise and good bombers over in Europe and Japan. He was stuck at the base on permanent party and was assigned to only train the cadets, and never experienced the war beyond the United States. His most memorable/ scary experience is that one day he was teaching the cadets how to drop bombs out the plane, and he almost fell through the hole in the plane where you drop the bombs.

5. What was everyday life like for Earl? Was he homesick a lot? How were his living conditions at camp? Was the food there good? How was he treated at camp?

Earl would live off camp with me in a bare room that was very basic and was a room and a bathroom. The room was somewhat like a shed. He was not homesick due to me being there, however, we would trade shifts, due to the different jobs we had. We would eat lamb and the food was very scarce. Everything that we needed or had was rationed and was hard to come by if you ran out of it due to the war occurring. Earl was treated with much respect at the training camp, due to being a corporal, and the citizens just respected all army men.

6. Do you remember V-J day and how did Earl react?

Victory over Japan day, Earl and I were getting a crib for our baby boy, and were nervous because Earl was to travel to Shepard field, Texas to find out where he was going to be shipped in Japan. We were on leave in Los Angeles and were trying to enjoy the rest of our day. On the bus home, sirens went off and we were so happy because we had learned that the war was over and were ecstatic that Earl wasn't going to have to go over due to having a family. Earl was extremely happy that day, however, I sensed some sadness within him due to the loss of good men during the war.

My Grandfather:

Matthew Gerlits

Fr. Jack Clark (I interviewed my grandma about what she had been told about my great uncle)

Great Uncle

4/21/12

I chose this person for my interview because he is my great uncle. I had heard it served during WW2 and is now a priest so he interested me even more. Interview

1. What were you doing before you joined the war?
   He was going to Loyola High school in Los Angeles and worked at a radio company as recommended by a Loyola priest so that he would have experience to get a good job in the military. After he was drafted he completed college via mail while on a Navy ship. He graduated from polytechnic. He lived at home and had no sweetheart.

2. Did you enlist or were you drafted?
   He was drafted into the war but had experience has a radio technician

3. Where did you go during the war?

   He was 1st stationed in San Diego as a radio technician. During the war he was later sent to the pacific front on supply ships. There was a treaty between the countries of WW2 not to attack supply ships but the Japanese often broke this treaty and attacked supply ships though he never saw battle.

4. What were you doing during the war?
   During the war he worked as part of the communication team as a radio technician. He never saw combat

5. Did you come home on leave? Yes he often came home on leave because he was station in San Diego which was close to his home at the time.

6. What was it like after the war?
   After the war he took advantage of the GI program and went to LMU and afterwards went to a Jesuit seminary and became a priest at the age of 33.

Ian Desdune

Mr. line

Period 5, World Hist 2

27 April 2012

Google Generation Q&A

Student: Ian Desdune

Veteran/Civilian Interviewed: Beria Loretta Forney

Relationship to the Student: Great Grandmother

Date and location: April 25th over the phone

Q. Where did you go during the war?

A. When Pearl Harbor took place I was a senior in high school. Everyone was somewhat scared, however we all knew America would win.

Q. What were you doing during the war?

A. Once the war started my mother did not want me to go to college, she wanted me to stay and work for the government and war, which was something pretty much all who were able to work did. My husband who I was not married to yet did not go to war because he helped build bombs for the army at Wright Aeronautical, which still exists in Daytona. Never knew anyone that served. I worked at a machine shop making tools until I married.

Q. What was everyday life like?

A. Food was now given in rations and supplies were not always given in abundance do to military needs. However, nothing really changed about the way she lived. People back then were a lot less tense and a lot nicer to each other. Everyone got along and no one complained we all did our part.

Q. What did you do to past time?

A. Time didn't really need to be pasted I worked went to movies and the basic things anybody did when the war was not going on.

Q. What was life like after the war?

A. After the war technology really started to change. I remember TVs just came out and we got one. My favorite shows were children shows. Phones then were not how they are today too. Unless you needed a phone you could not have one without a permit. Because my mother had a stroke I needed a phone to check on her during work. The bill was $3.85, to bad its not that now.

Q: Do you remember V-E Day and V-J Day when the war ended?

A: "I just remember hearing on the radio that we had won the war in Europe and Japan and people were screaming THE WAR IS OVER!"

Q: How did you celebrate the end of the war?

A: "We didn't really celebrate the end of the war because my parents weren't the celebrating type."

Steven Chaves

Jacqueline Patricia Nicholson- Sacco

Grandmother

April 20, 2012

I thought my grandmother, an Italian American, was a perfect fit for this project because she lived during World War II. I don't know anyone who actually fought in the war and she is the only living person close enough to me to share her personal thoughts, feelings, and experience during this great time. She lost close friends, her life style changed drastically, and memory of this historical time.

Q: During the war did you have to move?

A: "Yes. Until 1942 I lived in a two story six bedroom, two bathroom house in New Jersey. When we moved out here I lived in a one bedroom apartment and shared a bathroom with six other people."

Q: Did you have any prize possessions during this time?

A: "When I was 5 my grandmother gave me a 1942 doll that I took everywhere."

Q: Did you lose any of your friends during the war?

A: "My cousin fought in the war. He was a fighter pilot that was shot down near the English war was over and was never the same. He became an alcoholic and eventually committed suicide."

Student: Pablo Casillas
Civilian Interviewed: Elsa Lujan
Relationship: Grandmother
Date of Interview: May 22, 2012
Location: Students House

World War II was one event in our history that affected most parts of the world especially Europe, Asia, and the United States. However, what about the other countries and nations that weren't involved as much like Mexico, South America, and other countries and nations. By interviewing my grandmother I can see how people lived in Mexico during that time period, and whether it affected how the people lived. I could also find out if Mexico did anything to help the war. Through this interview I will understand how it affected the Mexican society. Lastly, I would like to find out her views on the war and if Mexico could have done more.

Interview:

1. From whom or what did you get the news of World War 2?
   - The first time I heard about World War II was when my father was listening to his radio in the store he had. I also remember that all my neighbors and my dad's friends would gather to listen to the news.

2. Was World War II a common topic to be talking about around your town?
   - Yes, many of the people in my town would speak about World War II. However, the people were speaking with fear because they felt the war was spreading all over Europe, and somehow it could go into the U.S and other nations. The main source of the fear also came from Hitler's massive genocides he was starting.

3. Did you ever see any propaganda from the United States to get people into war?
   - Yes, there was propaganda that the U.S was using in Mexico. The main source where they used propaganda was in the newspaper called "El Universal". I also remember that they would have cartoons that had Hitler, Mussolini, and Hirohito.

4. Do you remember if Mexico sent any soldiers to the war over seas?
   -I remember that Mexico sent the squadron 201 from Mexico, that were air force pilots and they helped in bombing.

5. Do you believe Mexico could have done more during the war?
   - I believe that Mexico has always tried to stay away from war, and has tried to remain a peaceful nation. They have always tired to use their army to have peace, and I believe that Mexico sent the best that they could give to the war.

Alex Peck
Interviewing: Martha Katz
Connection: Grandma
Phone interview

I chose to interview my grandma because she was alive during World War II. She visits from Massachusetts a couple times a year and she has a vivid remembrance of the WWII era. We have a very close relationship and it was fun to interview her.

How old were you when u found out about the war?
      I was 8 years old, born in 1936. Found out about it in 1943-1944.

Did you know anyone who fought in the war?
      Yes, I remember being at school in 4th or 5th grade when someone's older brother came home on leave. Her brother was 18. People lied about their ages to be able to enlist and go fight for their country. There was a lit if patriotism running through their blood.

How did the war affect you and your family?
      I wasn't too affected. I lived in the country on a farm, and a couple of cousins went over to fight. No one in my immediate family was in service. We used to go to grocery store and things were rationed, because soldiers needed supplies. She remembers margarine became more popular than butter. Only limited gasoline for car.

How did you feel when you found out about the war?
      Communication was limited, so the news didn't reach where I lived until much later. Letters were delivered and took months be delivered. I thought Franklin D. Roosevelt would take care of it. I thought the president was wonderful and that he would do everything he could to take care of his country.

What was your reaction to Pearl Harbor?
      I can't really remember that, but my husband remembers hearing about it on a Sunday, and he felt it was inconceivable. He felt that it was completely uncalled for, and he compared it to present day's 9/11 on a larger scale.

Student: Sam Raycraft
Veteran/Civilian Interviewed: Jerry Clark
Relationship to the student: Neighbor
Date and location of the interview: April 21, 2012; Altadena, CA

I chose Mr. Clark because he lives across the street from me. We have always had a good relationship and I am friends with his grandchildren. He is very knowledgeable and likes to share stories from his past. Mr. Clark has always struck me as a peculiar man and I have wanted to get to know him more and hear about his past. This project allowed me to ask questions about him personally and hear interesting stories about WWII.

1. What were you doing before you joined the military?

Living in Charleston, SC going to high school. I dropped out of high school to join the service in September of 1939. At this time Germany had just invaded Poland and I waited until I turned 17 at the end of the month before I could enlist.

3. Did you enlist or were you drafted?

I enlisted because it was before the draft took place. Most of the guys I hung around with were in their 20s or 30s, I didn't like school and was a little rebellious, so this was a way to get out of school and see the world. I chose the Navy because we lived on the big Navy base that was located in Charleston. My father was a quarter master (supply sergeant) in the Marines

6. What were you doing during the war?

Initially when I got in the service I was a photographer on minesweepers that went through harbors trying to make mines explode. My job was to take pictures of the mines so we could find ways to detonate new mines in a safer way. After that I went on patrol planes in the Atlantic that were looking for enemy submachines and I would take pictures of them. Late in the war I went into training to become a frog man (Underwater Demolition Team). I was going to go take pictures of the UDT blowing obstructions up. This was when the US was preparing to invade Japan and they needed soldiers to either blow up obstructions or diffuse mines along the Japan coastline so tanks and trucks could go inland. Since the war ended right before we invaded Japan, I never had to go abroad. Luckily I didn't because 9 out of 10 UDT soldiers would die because of the dangerous nature of the job they were doing. They also could easily be shot at because they were in swimsuits and the only weapon they carried was a knife.

9. What was your every day life like?

I didn't meet my wife until after the war, so I wasn't overly attached to anyone at home. I sent letters to my mother and father back in Charleston on occasion, as did my mother to me. I was never really homesick though. I was ready to leave and I didn't feel much attachment to my home. Food was bleak in taste and at times we didn't have enough. After America joined the war in '41 we felt the effects of rationing that our families were feeling at home. I had it better though, being as I wasn't abroad. We lived on regular barrack bunks with dozens of fellow soldiers. Equipment, just like food, started to be harder to come by after '41 because the resources were being stretched much thinner.

13. What was it like after the war?

After the war I went back home to Charleston, but there was not much work for service men at that time. A couple buddies and I moved up to Iowa to work on a Chicken farm belonging to a family friend. After a while I got tired of that and took a job at Sears taking pictures of babies. When I was in Iowa I met my wife and we got married. A few years after the war ended I rejoined the Navy because I couldn't take any more crappy jobs. I went on "detachments" to China, Manchuria, Guam, and Greece after the war as a part of work groups. I was a part of the occupying force that was in Manchuria after the war for a few months. Around 1948, not long after I had my son, I was coming home from a job in Alaska and I was taken off the flight at the last minute because an Officer pulled rank. The plane ended up crashing and killing everyone on it. In 1950 I was stationed down in Pensacola, FL working in a hangar on an air force base. In the hangar they were simulating what it would be like to live and work in Antarctica. I retired from the Navy in 1960 at which point I got my GED. After getting out of the military for the second time I got a job in Columbus, OH at North American Aviation working on a camera system for the X15 rocket plane. The X15 was used to see what it would be like for astronauts going to space so it flew really high in the atmosphere. I left there after a year to go back to Florida, where I worked at a movie company that made commercials, shot football games, and made military training films. Later I worked at RCA making circuit boards for Apollo 4. In 1970 I got my AA in Hotel and Restaurant Management, but since it was so long after the war I was not able to get any benefits from the GI Bill. From 1970 to 1990 I worked at motels as a night manager, and other odd jobs, while moving back and forth across the state.

Jerry Clark, 1941

Student: Tristan Wilkerson

Veteran/Civilian Interviewed: Grandmother in place for Grandfather

Relationship to the student: Grandmother

Date and Location of the interview: 4/16/12 across the phone

I choose to interview my grandmother because she was the closest to my grandfather who served in World War II. Even though she was a civilian at the time, She gained knowledge of what was happening in the war through her husband via letter. My Grandfather wrote to her everyday talking about each other's day went and the adventures each day held.

Q: Do you remember how you felt about Japan or the war in Europe prior to Pearl Harbor?
A: They had huge headlines in the newspaper, but I don't recall much. I had no idea what Pearl Harbor was. It did scare everybody though. I remember President Franklin D. Roosevelt going on the news declaring war on Japan. Mainly ignorance and fear of the war was what I was feeling.
Q: Did you write many letters home? Did people write to you? What did you want to say?
A: I wrote many letters, as he wrote back everyday. We talked about everything and anything that happened that day. Even though I was very busy, I still took the time to write back 5-6 times a week.
Q: What was the food like?
A: The food was chipped beef on toast, which was basically salted beef on toast. Their nickname for it was sheep "crap" on a shingle.
Q: Were there times when you felt homesick or stressed?
A: He felt homesick everyday and missed me (my grandmother) very much.
Q: Did you go to school? Did you take advantage of the GI Bill?
A: Yes, He got his tuition paid off and got 75$ a month, also an athlete scholarship for track and basketball. If you were married, you got 105$ and 115$ if you had a child. Books and supplies were paid for but stopped after the Korean War begun. Many veterans went back to serve but he stayed to get married to me.
Q: What were you doing during the war?
A: I remember the Blackouts we had. We had to put out all lights so that bombers wouldn't see the city overhead and pass by. Loud sirens came to warn you when a bomber was near by and wardens would walk the streets to make sure everyone had all light off and checked each of the houses.
Q: Can you tell me about your most memorable experiences?
A: My most memorable experience was at the Baltimore train station. We arrived by streetcar and he left on the train very slowly waving goodbye. His departure to the war and when he returned were my most memorable times. He was gone for 18 months then came back and graduated college where he began his teaching career in New Orleans.

David S. Williams III
Interviewed David S. Williams Jr. on behalf of David S. Williams Sr.
Father on behalf of my late grandfather
April 20, 2012 email correspondence

I chose my father as the person for me to interview because he had told me stories about my grandfather's time in World War II. I was close to my Grandfather, but in September of 2000 he passed away. During the summer I would go to Minnesota to visit my grandparents, and Ompi, my grand father, would go fishing with me. I spent a lot of time with him, and I was very fond of him.

1) Did Ompi enlist, or was he drafted? If he enlisted, why and where?

He was drafted, and went into the Army at the age of 18.

2) Where was Ompi stationed and what was the trip there like?

He was in training in Texas and became very ill. About that time the war was ending, and he went by ship to Europe and by train to Germany, riding in a boxcar, unable to change out of his uniform or even remove his boots during the three-day train trip to Wiesbaden, where he was a glider mechanic.

3) What was Ompi doing during the war? What were his jobs and assignments?

As a glider mechanic he helped maintain and launch gliders behind propeller planes. He saw a man cut in half when the cable snapped before take-off, he also saw a fellow soldier run over by a jeep.

4) What was Ompi's daily life like? Did he write letters to people/did people write to him? What were living conditions like?

He lived on the top floor of a building in Wiesbaden and during the winter it got so cold one night the pipes burst, and they fixed the pipes with chewing gum.

He was cold that winter, he didn't drink or smoke, and would give his cigarettes to fellow soldiers.

He wrote and received many letters from family and friends. He was never sick while stationed in Germany, only in Texas before he was commissioned.

Since he didn't drink, apparently he spent a lot of time in his barracks sleeping.

5) Did Ompi belong to any veteran organizations? Did he go to any reunions with them?

I am not aware of any Army-related veteran organizations that he belonged to, but he did become a member of the Coast Guard Auxiliary in Minnesota. In later life he joined Kiwanis, which is a service organization dedicated to helping the poor, but not related to the military.

To my knowledge he never again saw any of the men with whom he served, nor did he attend any Army-related reunions.

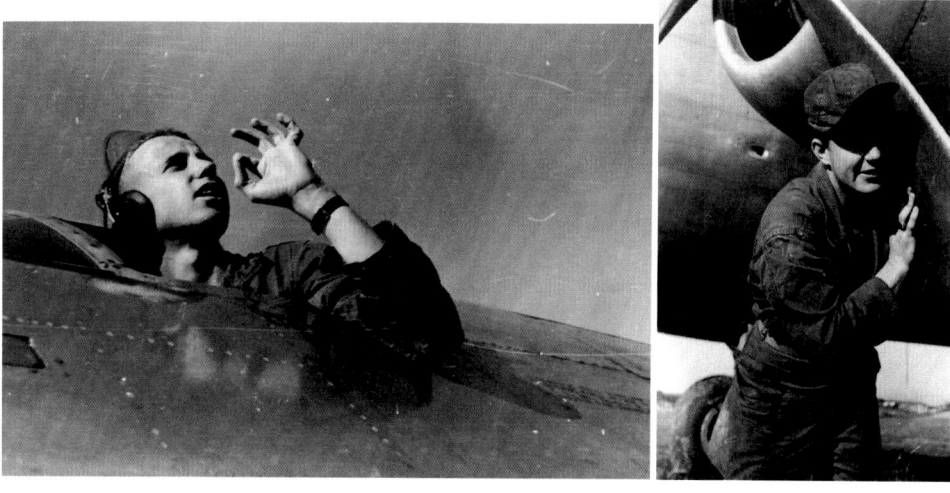

Student: Nick Zoppi
Veteran Interviewed: Christopher Stefano
Relationship: Grandfather
April 19, 2012, Manhattan Beach, CA

        I chose to interview my grandfather because he was alive during the time of WWII, even though he didn't serve at the time. He told me stories of the days he was in the Navy, and I knew he would be the one I would interview for this project, for he was the only one who served in my family.

What were you doing before you joined the military?

        Where were you living?
        -Living in Jersey City
        Were you attending school?
        -No
        Did you have a Sweetheart?
        -Yes: Grandma

2.Do you remember how you felt about Japan or the war in Europe prior to Pearl Harbor?

        I was a young boy, and didn't realize about Pearl Harbor until I was 6 years old. I was Born in '37 and Pearl Harbor in '41. I was 4 years old at the time. It was on my mother's birthday.
        Do you remember the day Pearl Harbor was attacked?
      -December 7th, 1941
        Were you able to meet famous war heroes of the time?
      No.

3 Did you enlist or were you drafted?

        -Enlisted
        What motivated you to enlist?
        -Growing up during war years, patriotism, career came after WWII, Propaganda and glory, movies didn't show how terrible war was. Showed people dying but didn't show the horror. Senator McCarthy and communism.
        From the day he was 17. Uncle was in the navy.
        Did any friends enlist with you?
       -    Ramon went in the army around same time. And Bobby Paine went in the army.
          Where did you go to join?
       -    Went into the reserves in 1955, January, went on act of duty in Oct. 1955
          Why did you choose the Navy?
       -    Clean living and beds, Uncle was influence
          What did you envision it would be like after you joined?
       -    Seeing the world

4. What do you remember about your first days in the military?

        -First night at boot camp, all young, people crying, didn't understand why.
        Do you remember anything from boot camp?
        -Boot camp in Bainbridge Maryland
        How did it feel?
        -Felt nervous when he heard the guys crying, became kind of funny, looked forward to the drills
        Was it hard?
        -Conditioning was hard in beginning, a lot of marching and building strength.
        Do you remember anything about your instructor?-Boilermaker was in charge of company; he was in company 59 5th platoon

5. What do you remember about the other people in your unit?

    -Racism, southerners didn't like the blacks, no close friends.
    -Liked the officers, except Chief Warrant Officer.

before the war he didn't have a job or a house. After the war ended he had a sense of accomplishment and happiness.

Henry James Bailey Senior

Born in January 7, 1911 and Died January 25, 1999

Place of birth: Norco Louisiana

Job in WW2: Cook and Supply Depoe Clerk

Station: Fort Bliss originally known as Camp Bliss in El Paso Texas

Relationship to me: Great Grandfather

Interviewee: Grandson Woodrow Edward Bailey Junior

Interview with my Veteran

1. What were you doing before you joined the military? He was doing odd jobs because there were no opportunities for men back during that time. It was during the Great Depression. He did not finish high school and was living in Gonzales Louisiana. He met his sweet heart a little before World War 2 broke out. Her name was Anna Bell Ransom. He was already enlisted in the army before the war but was deactivated because there was no need for him. When WW2 broke out he was reactivated.

2. Did you enlist or were you drafted? He enlisted in the Army and was stationed in El Paso Texas. A few of his friends did enlist with him but he was the first of his friends to do so. When he enlisted he enlisted with the Army in the 1930's because in the Army he felt that he could actually help and be a part of the war. It was a unique experience to him mainly because he really thought that he could help serve his country and make a difference.

3. What were you doing during the war? He was a supply Depoe Clerk and a cook. His job was to cook all the meals during the day or whatever time was his shift. His other job was to keep track of all the equipment and made sure that everyone had the proper gear and knew how to use it. His most memorable experience during the war was when he was having his fifth child during the time he was serving his country he had to petition his commanding officer to let him leave the army during a short period of time so that he could see his fifth child being born. The commanding officer thought he was one of the leaders were he was stationed so he had no problem letting him take a short absence so he could witness another of his kids being born.

4. Were you awarded any medals or citations? He was awarded one citation for exemplary service and was awarded some medals but couldn't remember where they were or what they were for. He always strides to do his best and be the best at whatever he was doing. The awards and medal meant a lot because he got to serve his country. Besides getting married and having kids this was one of his greatest memories of his life.

5. What was it like after the war? After the war he got the GI Bill that allowed him to buy the house that he always wanted and he lived in the house for 50 years. He was also very happy to have served his country in the way that he did. He had more children and got a pretty good job and lived the rest of his life in the way that he wanted which was important to him because

Paul Calfo
Private Alexander Artzer
April 20, 2012

The Greatest Google Generation

I chose to interview my father about my great grandfather because he was a family role model who I knew had served in World War II. My father always talked about him, so I knew he had some interesting stories to tell.

Me : What was Grandpa doing before he joined the military?

Dad: Grandpa worked on a farm in Sterling, Colorado, where he would load and unload farm equipment, seed, and produce from ages 8-18. He knew what hard work really was. The whole while, he was attending high school.

Me: Did he enlist or was he drafted?

Dad: My grandpa was drafted, and reported in Denver, Colorado.

Me: Where did he go during the war?

Dad:Before my grandpa actually went into the battlefield, he went to Rialto, California, as part of the 622nd Division. He was put into a company which the army used, where virtually everyone in the group had worked on a farm. There were about 240 men originally in the company. The company's job was loading and unloading munitions onto railcars that would go to the Port of Los Angeles. It was extremely hard and difficult work. They picked the men specifically because of their ability to handle hard work. These munitions included rockets and photoflash, and photoflash was a type of pre-bomb that could be shot off at night, and once it exploded in mid air, troops could see at night. The munitions would then go onto the ships to be shipped out to the Pacific (this is after he had basic training in Yuma, Arizona). He stayed in Rialto for 9 months. The army then moved the 622nd Division to the Pacific Theatre. In November, 1943, the whole division was sent to San Francisco. They boarded a ship, left San Francisco, and the last thing my Grandpa remembered was when he left San Francisco, he left the Golden Gate Bridge crying. Tears came into his eyes because he did not know what to expect when he would confront the Japanese, and he didn't know if he would come back home. Several weeks passed on the ship. He became anxious. My grandpa told my father about one example where the men were very hungry, and my Grandpa's best friend in the 622nd, Orville Potter, asked for more beans during dinner. On a typical evening, the division was feeding all the troops beans with one serving each, and when they finished feeding the troops, they threw the remaining beans overboard. Then, Orville Potter said, "I want more beans!" The commanding officer said, "That's a no go", and threw the beans overboard; even after that, Orville had to respond to the commanding officer for punishment. Orville was forced to scrub the deck. After a couple months, the 622nd arrived in Australia. The Japanese were bombing Australia as the troops arrived, so the 622nd, a support division, helped fight. They helped the army support the Australians while the Japanese bombed the coast. My Grandpa was there for a couple of weeks, supporting the Australians, but then he was shipped to New Guinea. He then helped fight the Japanese off of the island. Not only did my Grandpa help fight the Japanese, but he took a skip loader and moved the munitions all around New Guinea for the troops. Once the army finally beat the Japanese on New Guinea, they celebrated, but was then sent to the Phillipines. They fought in the Phillipines, and the 622nd was there when Douglas McArthur landed, once they defeated the Japanese. There were 138 troops left from the original 240.

Me: What was his every day life like?

Dad:My grandpa's job was not only to help fight the Japanese, but he took a skip loader and moved the munitions all around New Guinea around the troops. he had to help hide them from the Japanese when not in use. They would move along with the army troops, witnessing death by the thousands.

Me: What did he do to pass the time?

Dad:He played cards when he was not fighting, practice shooting targets, and he would reminisce on America and think about his family and girlfriend back home. He always wrote letters to his family. The living conditions were often humid, hot, and dirty. There was barely enough food to go around. One of the experiences he held dear to himself was when he had thought he heard Japanese bombers fly over while eating dinner; he had never seen so many kids who declared they were Atheists make the sign of the cross.

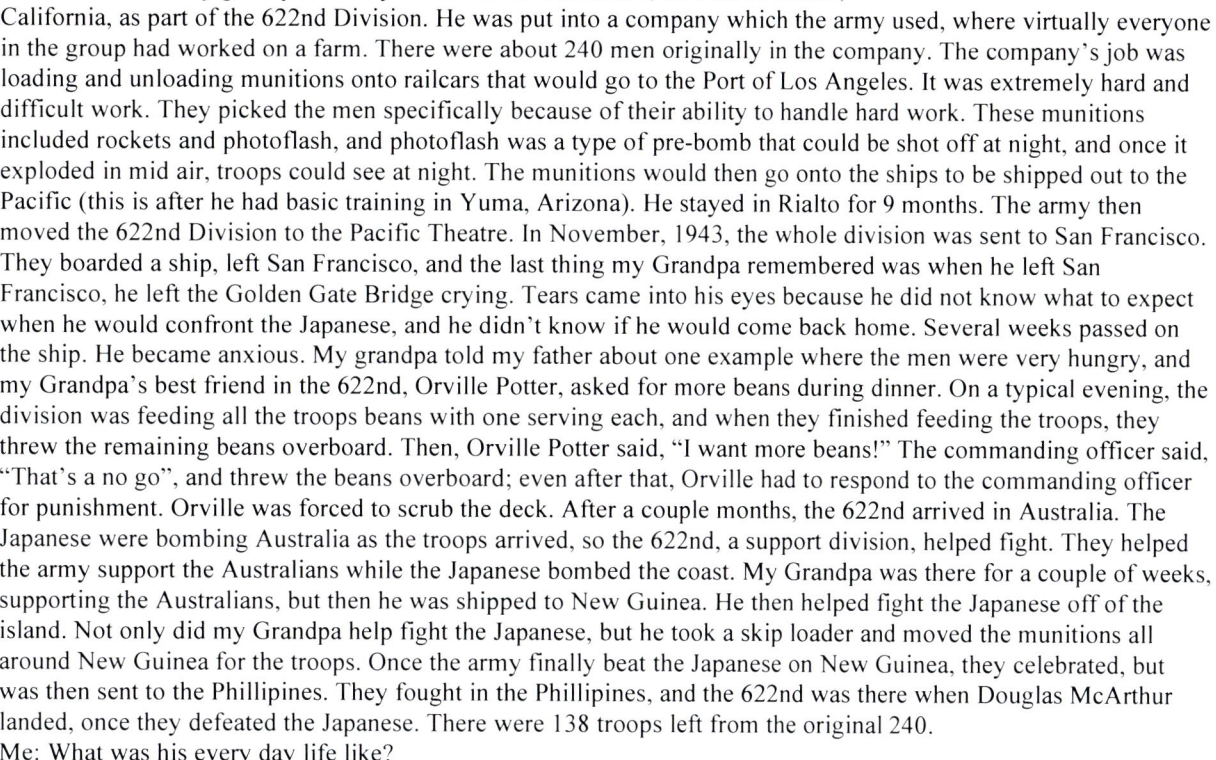

THE AMERICAN HOMEFRONT

Life on the home front during World War II was a significant part of the war effort for all participants and had a major impact on the outcome of the war. The United States became involved with new issues such as rationing, manpower allocation, home defense, and evacuation in the face of air raids. The American Home front came together to help our boys win the war on two fronts.
These are the stories from those who were there...

Student: Michael Willoughby

Where were you during World War 2?

"I was born on the island of Cebu and later I moved Manilla as a young teen. I stayed in Manila during the majority of World War two and I also remember the battle of Manila in (doesn't remember date)

What do you remember about the Battle of Manila?

I remember the invasion of the Japanese and the extensive fighting. Luckily I ran away with a group of my friends to the hills. I remember hiding in the mountains and hearing babies cry.

And how old were you at this time?

16 years old. I remember, it was two years before I met Benard (husband)

How scared were you in those caves?

"Boy, you don't even know what scared is. The cave was real damp and really cramped. We were too scared to leave in fear we would get spotted. I remember one of my friends left the cave and she never came back. (crying)"

How did you know when it was safe to leave?

American troops found our cave after the 4th day. I don't know how we survived but we just did.

Were you relocated? I know the battle lasted for a month in Manila.

Yes we were relocated to an outskirt city protected by the United States. After the war ended, it was there that I fell in love with Bernard.

What were you doing at the time of the war?

I was working at a Mini mart in Manila. I was still in high school but my job was a cash register.

Do you remember any fighting before the invasion of Manila?

"No I don't, you know I have somewhat a bad memory."

Do you remember much about Bernard? What division he was a part of?

"No I can't remember. It was so long ago and I just forgot these things"

I remember a couple days ago we talked about the caves, do you remember how many people were with you?

"It was me, three of my friends (girls) and about 5 older guys. There was this family with a newborn baby that I could never forget because he would never shut up. Haha."

Steven Reed
Mrs. Alice Irvine and Mr. Thomas Irvine
Neighbors
April 20, 2012/ The Irvine Residence, Los Angeles, CA

After a long search, which included asking several people over the age of 60 what they knew about WWII, I learned that my neighbors' uncle was captured by Japanese soldiers and was a prisoner of war for over four years. The Irvines gladly agreed to let me interview them, and Mrs. Irvine shared very vivid memories and details during our time together.

1. Where were you and your family living before your uncle became involved in the war?
   -My family and I were living in Los Angeles when the war started, we had moved from Arizona in August of 1941.

2. Did your uncle enlist or was he drafted?
   -Well, neither of those happened exactly. My uncle, Albert Freese, was a government employee that was in Wake Island working on bridges to connect the three islands of Okinawa when Pearl Harbor was bombed. The government issued every worker there a rifle, whether or not they had ever been trained, let alone held a gun. My uncle was lucky because he used to hunt, so he was pretty handy with guns. Unfortunately, the men that were working there were all captured.

3. How were you and your family affected by the news that your uncle was captured and had become a prisoner of war?
   -We were all devastated. From the time we got the news of his capture, until the time he came home, the entire family worried about him.

4. Did your uncle ever tell you what everyday life was like for him while he was a prisoner?
   -He never told me directly but I always listened from the other room when he told my parents. He said that life was very difficult and very scary. The patrol officers would often beat and injure prisoners, and would send them back to the barracks without treatment. The prisoners were forced to wake up at 3 o'clock in the morning to exercise and work in the coal mines. Because they had to work well past sunset, my uncle did not see the light of day for over 4 years.

5. How did your uncle manage to survive all of this?
   -It's simple: He survived on rice and seaweed, which was all prisoners were given, from the time he was captured until he was set free over four years later. My Uncle said he also did his best to stay out of trouble and make the best of his situation. Even after all he has been through, my uncle still had no animosity towards any of the Japanese people who treated him so poorly.

Mr. and Mrs. Irvine

Uncle Albert returned home
at a weight of only 98 pounds

Aaron Villalobos

Mr. Line

World History 2, Period 5

26 April 2012

WWII Veteran Interview—Brice Martin

Brice Martin served in the navy during World War II and was stationed in places such as Okinawa and Guam. Brice was nineteen years old when he enlisted in the navy and went to Manuel Arts High School in Los Angeles at the time of the war. He decided to enlist in the navy because it seemed the most appealing to him. He figured the navy would offer a good supply of food and always a good place to rest. In 1942 he went to enlist at age 19 into the navy. He went through extensive physical examination and ended up in the marine raiders. He soon went into regular infantry and eventually became part of the sixth marine battalion in Okinawa. His job was to take care of wounded and sick soldiers. He wrote letters home primarily to his mother, father, and sister during his service but had to be careful not to reveal his location or any military objectives in his letters. Brice relatively had enough food during his service and never went starving. The food rations would often consist of cheese, dog biscuits, cigarettes, chocolate bars, vegetable stew, meat and bread. During his service he had to camp out in the wilderness of Okinawa and for him the environment was relatively stress free but there was the occasional ambush. Things got pretty intense during combat and Brice would have to treat any wounded soldiers after. Soldiers weren't allowed to bring things with them in the war but Brice managed to take photograph of a young lady from his high school and others had cameras with them. When the war ended Brice was in Okinawa and received news of the victory in Europe. It was December 1945 when Brice came home and he had spent two years overseas. He was very happy that the war had ended and decided to go back to school when he came home and was discharged in San Francisco. Upon returning home he and his comrades were happy to see their families and have their freedom. Brice was twenty-two when the war ended and continued living in Los Angeles. He went to USC and would eventually get married, move to Manhattan Beach, get a teaching job and go back to school and become a doctor. Today Brice is happily retired in Manhattan Beach.

Stephen Docherty
Peter Abundis
Grandfather
April 8, 2012 Ventura CA

        I choose to interview my grandfather, Peter Abundis, age 88, because he has lived a life full of inspiring experiences. I admire his heroism and find his stories about his family history and heritage fascinating. His stories include his recollection enlisting to serve our country during WWII to how he met and married with my grandmother while stationed in Hawaii. He recalls the events such as why he chose the Navy, his initial training, job duties and places visited during his 4-year tour of duty. He ended his tour of duty in Hawaii, meeting his future wife and marrying her prior to returning to the states.

Q: Did you enlist or were you drafted?
A: I enlisted in Downtown L.A.
Q: What motivated you to enlist?
A: The glamour that people spoke of to be in the navy.
Q: Did any friends enlist with you?
A: No.
Q: Where did you go to join?
A: I went to downtown L.A. to a recruiting office on Main Street.
Q: Why did you choose your branch of the service?
A: I joined the navy because the ladies loved sailors.
Q: What did you envision it would be like after you joined?
A: I envisioned that I would become a lady magnet.
Q: Where did you go during the war?
A: I went to Treasure Island and then I went to Hawaii.
Q: Where were you stationed first?
A: I was stationed at Treasure Island first.
Q: What do you remember when you first arrived at the new location?
A: I was nervous and scared at first because the bombing of Pearl Harbor had just happened.
Q: Did you travel to other places?
A: I visited other zones but I could not recall where the exact locations were.
Q: What were you doing during the war?
A: I was in the navy pay office.
Q: What jobs and assignments did you have?
A: I was assigned to process payroll.
Q: Did you see combat?
A: No.
Q: Can you tell me your most memorable experiences?
A: Meeting your grandmother.
Q: What do you remember about the other people in your unit?
A: I do not remember much, one guy was stuck up and some of the guys acted like they were in a frat.
Q: Did you have any close friends?
A: No I was an individualist.
Q: What did you think of your officers?
A: I did not think very much about them because there were not fascinating.
Q: Were there casualties in your unit?
A: No.
Q: Were you awarded any metals or citations?
A: Yes I was awarded a form duty medal.
Q: How did you earn them?
A: Through foreign duty and hard work.
Q: What do the medals mean to you?
A: Not very much close to nothing.
Q: What do you hope to do with these medals?
A: I do not have hope for these medals.

Youtube LinkPt1:
http://www.youtube.com/watch?v=4cOQLETa8oE&context=C47f43d2ADvjVQa1PpcFN9z079QRHDPnoxcfP5T8GKMSGYaSRz87o=

Student: Chris Franco
Civilian Interviewed: Richard Chacon
Relationship to the Student: Grandfather
Date and Location of Interview: 4/24/2012, home

I chose to interview my Grandfather Richard Chacon because he knows the most about his stepfather, Walter Balicki, a World War II veteran. Walter rarely discussed his experiences in the war with us while he was still alive, and I was too young to notice what he had experienced. When my parents or grandparents did bring it up, he would refuse to talk about it. We will always remember him as a kind-hearted and gentle man.

Q: What was he doing before he joined the military?

A: When he was in high school he played on his high school softball team. We don't know the name of his high school, but their mascots were the Ambassadors. He was a centerfielder and was a pretty good player. We found out that he played in a tournament at Loyola High School! At the time, Loyola's field was known as "Loyola Stadium," and Wally was published in the several articles during that tournament.

Q: What was he doing during the war?

A: Walter was an air force photographer of war on a B-24 Liberator. He was in charge of photographing sites that had been previously bombed in order to acquire a damage assessment and other valuable information about those sites. Occasionally, he would switch places with the door gunner and use the 12.7 mm Browning machine gun.

Q: Where did he go during the war?

A: He was first stationed at a naval base on the island of Guam in 1944. From there, he would go out on his flight tours in the B-24 to take photographs. Based on his photos, much of his time at Guam was like a paradise vacation. He once mentioned fighting on the front-lines very briefly, but refused to speak of it any further.

Q: Was he awarded any medals or citations?

A: We do know that he was awarded several medals, and articles were written to honor his heroic deeds. Unfortunately, we do not know the specific details of these awards or articles.

Q: What was life like for him after the war?

A: After the war Walter came to appreciate the things that he was missing while he was deployed such as home and family. He became more open and friendly in contrast to his seriousness and closed disposition which he displayed before the war. His former sweetheart had broken up with him while he was away, so he eventually came to marry our Great Grandmother, my Grandfather Richard's mother.

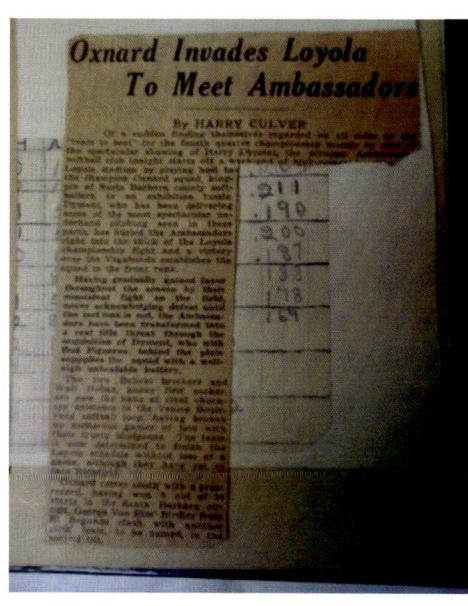

Student: Christopher M. Laun
Veteran/Civilian Interviewed: Florence O'Brien
Relationship to the student: Grand Aunt
Date and Location of the Interview: 4/23/12 Phone interview

My Auntie Flo is a civilian who grew up in the Philippines during World War II. She lived in Manila, and has many stories about living in the red zone. Ever since I was young, she has told me numerous stories about how life was like during the war. One of the scariest stories was about her encounter with a Japanese Sniper. One night she was eating dinner with her family, and invited a couple of American GI's to eat with them. About half an hour later, one of the GI's heard a noise outside, and told everyone to quiet down. My Aunts sisters walked into her room, and opened the window and saw the Japanese sniper with a grenade in his hand, ready to throw it into the house. Thankfully, one of the American soldiers outside saw the Japanese sniper, and shot him before he could do any harm. At the time, my aunt was only 15 years old, and still remembers the emotions and thoughts running through her head as this took place. Every time she tells me stories about the war, I realize just how dangerous it can be to live on the front lines.

Interview Questions

1. Where were living when the war began?

- "I was living in Manila. The day was December 8th, and the reason I remember this is because I remember going to my cousins birthday party, and heard the news of the airport being bombed."

2. How old were you when the war started?

- "I was only 15 years old when the war started."

3. What was your every day life like?

- "It was tough with the Japanese being so cruel. I remember the Province giving food to the civilians at the beginning of the war, and then the Japanese capturing it and taking all of the food. My family planted vegetables in the garden to eat, but we needed to plant more because of the food shortages."

4. What was it like living under Japanese occupation?

-"I remember the Japanese being very cruel. One day the japanese came through the town, and my father was taken to a concentration camp In Santa Thomas (Santa Thomas University that was converted by the Japs) and was forced to work there for 3 years. When he was at the camp, I remember meeting a Japanese soldier that was born in the Philippines. He allowed us to meet and bring canned goods to my father, but only when he was on guard. When he wasn't there, the Japanese soldiers took the food that was meant for my father."

5. What was it like when the Americans liberated you from the Japanese?

- "One day my sister woke up and saw soldiers with German looking helmets pointing their guns at her house. She got dressed, and walked outside after realizing that they were American soldiers. She put her hands up saying, "Don't shoot me. I'm an American. I just want to know if my father is okay." They said where was your father? She said he was at the Santa Thomas concentration camp. The soldiers told her that the camp had been liberated, and that survivors were at the hospital. When we found out my father was okay, we were very relieved."

6. What was it like after the war?

- "After the war ended, businesses started up again, and schools started up, but I didn't go to school for a whole year after the war. After the war, things started to get back to normal, but everything felt different. People were so used to being hungry, and it was tough to get back on your feet."

* James Taylor
* Matthew Horway Witteman
* Grandfather
* Taylor house on April 22, 2012

       I chose my Veteran because even though he is no longer with us, he served a rich service to this country that I thought would be more than suitable for this project. He was a good man, loyal husband, and fabulous lawyer and it would be nice to have his name be shared as a hero. The interview was done over the phone with my uncle, who as a child, was amazed by his fathers stories. They are accurate, filled with action, and will be a great part in this book.

Question #1: Were did you go during the war?

"I was assigned to a ship in the Pacific region, the USS Starlight. We were dispatched to various parts of the Pacific Ocean during the war, including the Philippines, New Caledonia, and other Islands. I received mid- shipment training which was ninety days long on the East Coast. I was shipped out right when the battle of Layette Gulf had begun. After that I was beached."

Question #2: What were you doing during the war?

"I was a gunnery officer on the USS Starlight and sometimes I would take on night watch, which was usually midnight to eight in the morning. I saw combat many times. My most memorable experience was when we herd that a kamikaze aircraft was headed our way and we could not do anything about it. We did not know what to do and the captain came on the loud speaker and read Psalm 23 and the Lords prayer. They were so close that we could see the pilots. We could see the plane and we started to say goodbye, when all of a sudden an American fighter came out of nowhere and shot them down.

Question #3: What was your everyday life like?

"Apart from when we came under attack or when we were engaged in battle, life was very much routine. The keeping up of the artillery was standard and apart from a couple night watches here and there, things were the same. I wrote not to often but when I did, it only explained my love for them and how much I missed them and wanted to see them soon. The food was good for the officers. The crew on our ship was African-American, and were taken good care of. We were always well supplied. Our living conditions were not all that bad. I shared a small cabin with one other officer. I was never really homesick and I always carried photos of my parents and brothers. I did not believe in any good luck charms or superstitions, I just prayed to God."

Question #4:Do you remember V-E Day and V-J Day when the war ended?

"I remember V-J Day very well. After the victory, my ship went to China for a couple months. After that I came home and partied for a couple days. The end of the war meant going back to civilian life. Others had a very hard time doing it, but I found it easy. The only thing I was worried about was being drafted later.

Questions #5: What was it like after the war?

"Life was pretty good after the war. My first memories of coming home was going out to celebrate with all my friends. After I got settled in, I began to work for my father in his blind factory and machine shop. A few years later I applied to USC law school where I attended with all tuition paid by the GI bill. I was also accepted at Harvard Law School but decided to stay in California. I later became a lawyer."

Student: Adam Pilapil
Veteran/Civilian Interviewed: Daryl Creighton (civilian and veteran), Madelyn Creighton (civilian), and Joseph Creighton (veteran)
Relationship to the veteran: Grandfather and Grandmother and Great-Grandfather respectively
Date and Location of Interview: April 23, 2012

I chose to interview my grandfather because I knew about all the passion that he had for the World War II time period. I also knew that he had charted the different battles that had taken place throughout the war, and he would have a lot of important information that he could enlighten me on. My grandfather also had a father who had fought in World War I, so I could ask my grandfather about both wars, and he could give me perspective on having a father that was in the military, and also a view from when my grandfather was in the military.

Q: Can you tell me about anybody that was in your family that was either part of WWI or WW2? (Daryl Creighton answered the first four questions)

A: My dad was part of the navy before World War I began, and during the time that Teddy Roosevelt decided to send the navy around the world in order to show the power of the US. He went over to Europe around 1917 when the US joined the war.

Q: Were there any specific battles that he was a part of or any stories that he brought back?

A: He was on a battleship and destroyer, and he told me about the several encounters that he had with German submarines. He was a gun captain, and one time some German submarines attacked him and his gun blew up. Why, I do not know? And he said that he was the only person on his fleet that survived that attack. And he woke up nine months later in a Norfolk hospital out of a coma.

Q: During the war and when you were in high school what information were you getting about the war, what was your everyday life like?

A: Well I followed the war just out of curiosity as a kid, and I specifically followed the German invasion of Russia, and on a map I pinned all the points on the map where they were going. On the day the war ended, I was delivering mail, and the whole city exploded in happiness and celebration. Hollywood was the place where people celebrated the most. When I was part of the military, I went through basic air force training, and they were going to send me to mechanics school, but then they gave me an opportunity to get out and I took it.

Q: What were your affiliations with World War II, even though you were young?

A: Well I grew up during the time that the Japanese bombed Pearl Harbor, and I was about 13 or 14, and I remember on December 8th when the Japanese came to Los Angeles, and most of there was lots of anarchy and most of the lights were turned off. [So the Japanese planes could not identify large populations.] When I was 18 I enlisted in the air force because I always wanted to fly in 1947, but they changed the minimum age to 21, so they offered me a release from the military and I took it.

Q: Do you remember V-J Day when the war ended? (Madelyn Creighton)

A: I was on Catalina Island and all the military people were in their housing. Well all the Island burst loose. All the service men were running freely all through the island. It was the most exciting and thrilling day, and how happy everybody was that V-J had finally come.

YouTube Link of the Entire Interview: http://www.youtube.com/user/wadlosh?feature=mhee

Justin Caruso
Henry Caruso
Grandpa
April 22, 2012 at my Grandpa's house

I chose to interview my grandpa because I look up to him for all the things he has achieved in his life and for the courage he had to go fight in the war. He is a role model and a hero to me.

My grandpa enlisted to fight in the war at the age of 17 because he wanted to fight for his country and contribute to our army. At this time he was living with his parents in Los Angeles. He enlisted to the navy air force after his close friend recommended that to him. He began taking air force classes at the University of Southern California with around twenty other people. His training was based out of Arizona and Texas where day by day he kept a log of his flights. He was able to pass all of the physical test due to his athletic abilities being on the track team at school. He and his squad fought on the coast of Saipan in a four-engine bomber plane. The living conditions during the war were not too good, they slept on cheap cots and never had much time to sleep due to fighting. For fun him and his buddies would go to Jap camps and walk around or fly planes low to the ground and enjoy the land. He made it out the war safe and began Dollar Rent a Car. From there on he has been a successful business man and lives happily with a wife and has three kids, one of which is my dad.

the grounds). Their walls were like tents - very primitive. Conditions could be difficult - often depending on the weather.

Question 5
<u>Were you awarded any medals or awards? If so which ones.</u>
She received one of the highest ranks awarded to a woman. Retired as a Lieutenant Colonel in the Air Force. After starting off as a nurse, she rose to a head nurse, then a supervisor & finally helped set up new hospitals. Anne just did her work really well and sort of quietly moved up the ranks

<u>Question 6 do you remember any first hand experience that she might have like combat or some noises she heard</u>
She vividly remembers holidays away. She was in New Delhi during Thanksgiving and Christmas and many Indians and Brits living in New Delhi would open their houses and invite some of the higher ranked service people in. She remembers seeing some local eating dog once and it really grossed her out b/c they used a lot of dogs to herd cattle on the farm

ANNA E. MISER 8/2
(Mrs. H. T. Hardin)

Conor Lydon
Mr. Line
World History Period 6
April 24, 2012

The Google Generation

Relationship to me: my friend's great-aunt's
Name is Anne Ellen Miser
Date of interview April 14, 2012
Born in Cottonwood Falls, Kansas on November 4, 1911.
Was married 2x (first husband died)
She was a Registered Nurse and volunteered for Nurses Corps just before
WWII. She trained at Fort Benning, Georgia

I chose to interview Anne Miser because I was asking my team mates if
anyone had a relative who fought or worked in WW2 and I asked my friend
Oscar and he said his Great aunt was a nurse. I think interviewing a nurse
is great because she gives a different perspective than a foot solider or
pilot.
Question 1
What do you remember about your first days in the War as a nurse?
Not all of the hospitals Anne was in were "state of the art". For example,
She was often in tropical places and they had to scrounge around for
anything to use as moisturizer on their skin.

Question 2
Where did you go during the War?
She served in the war theatres of India, Philippines, Okinawa & Morocco

Question 3
What was your specific jobs during the battle or after a battle?
She became a supervisor of a 100-bed hospital in New Delhi, India in
1942. Shortly before retirement in 1963-64, she was a supervisor of
military hospitals in the Midwest

Question 4
What was your everyday like? more specifically the living conditions and
food She remembers that they always carried chewing gum (Spearmint
and Double mint) & gave it away to the local poor kids. She sent home
beautiful silks and linens that her family had never enjoyed/could afford
before. The hospital in the Philippines was similar to our thought of what a
field hospital would be (they were built on wooden floors to get them up off

Student: McAuley Evans
Civilian/Veteran Interviewed: Patricia McAuley (Husband: Terrence Francis McAuley)
Relationship to the student: Grandmother
Date and location of interview: April 25, 2012 via phone

I chose my grandmother to interview because she had the closest relationship with my grandfather, Terry McAuley. Since she was a civilian during World War II, she experienced first hand the effects the war had on the people of the United States of America, as well as the men who fought to protect their country. My grandma recalls her husband coming back from the war a changed man, suffering from shell shock to the point where he could not even watch fireworks, for fear of being bombed.

2. Do you remember how you felt about Japan or the war in Europe prior to Pearl Harbor?
A. We didn't feel any way about anything before Pearl Harbor. The war in Europe was just like any other foreign conflict we hear about today, not getting much attention from us U. S. civilians. I can't remember clearly what exact time of day I heard about Pearl Harbor, but as soon as my family got wind of the incident, everyone in our society was up in arms, ready for a fight.

3. Did you enlist or were you drafted? (Veteran)
A. My husband, along with most his friends, enlisted into the armed forces as soon as the Pearl Harbor attacks occurred. Pearl Harbor motivated him to enlist, but I cant speak for him where exactly he went to enlist. My husband applied to be in the Marines, but because of a heart problem failed his physical inspection. After that he went home and rested for three days straight, in hopes to steady the beat of his heart and pass the inspection for the Navy. After he passed, he told me he tried not to think about what the war would be like, but kept his mind on the fact that he was doing something for the greater good of his country.

5. Where did you go during the war? (Veteran)
A. My husband was stationed in Guam and the Philippines. He told me that he enjoyed being in the ocean, and savored his time at sea on the trip to the South Pacific. Terry (veteran) had to stop traveling around half way through his service because of his heart problems. He used to black out frequently because of his heart problems, and this was especially dangerous as he was climbing up ladders on a regular basis and could have fallen and killed himself or others.

6. What were you doing during the war?
A. Terry (veteran) got assigned one of the most dangerous jobs there was in his division. When they arrived in the South Pacific, his ship, along with nine others, were given the job to motor near enemy gunships as decoys. Only three came back. One of the most memorable and scary experiences he told me about was when an American soldier froze at the gun as a kamikaze fighter approached his ship. Terry grabbed the gun out of the petrified soldier's hands, and saved all the men on his ship when he shot the left engine of the plane down.

9. What was everyday life like?
A. Everyday life during the war had the sense of something missing in America. MEN. We used to go the hospitals to volunteer for all the doctors who had been sent into the war as medics. We wanted to write to our family members in the war, but never got a chance to find out where exactly they were station, and mail was not something easily accessible in the South Pacific. There were times where my husband said he felt anxious to get home, because he had left his mother alone with 'The McAuley Cleaning Company'. My husband said the only thing to a 'superstition' that he had with him was God in the Navy. Terry (veteran) used to give a sermon even though he wasn't a priest to the men on his ship every Sunday on the open ocean. Although the conditions were tough, Terry said that he enjoyed being out in the ocean and was glad he ended up in the Navy

Bryce Roski-Amendola
Veteran interviewed: Edward Roski, Jr. about Edward Roski, Sr.
Relationship: great grandfather
Date and location: April 25, 2012

I interviewed my grandfather, Edward Roski, Jr. about my great grandfather, Edward Roski, Sr. I chose to discuss my great grandfather because he is my relative and actively participated in World War II. He fought in Asia after Pearl Harbor. He was in the navy and I was interested in knowing his story since he's my family.

Interview Questions:

1. What were you doing before you joined the military? *He was a salesman for the Oklahoma meat district.*

2. What motivated you to enlist? *Back then, everyone enlisted because it was a sign of patriotism. It was also a way to leave Oklahoma and see the world.*

3. Where did you go during the war? *He was one of the first people in China and landed in Shanghai. He was a gunner on the boat and was on the Yellow River when the war was won.*

4. What was every day life like? *It was mainly drills and preparation for battle.*

5. What was life like after the war? *He moved to California and opened a real estate business.*

EDWARD ROSKI, SR.

Student: Jonathan Sugianto

Veteran Interviewed: Teddy Johannes

Relationship to the student: Grandpa

Date and Location of the interview: April 22, 2012 (by phone)

I chose to interview my grandpa because he is a smart and noble man. Since he is a part of my family, I wanted to know what life was like back then and how he and his wife survived throughout his journey. Also chose my grandpa because he lives in Indonesia and I don't get to meet him very often. I think that if I understood his past and involvement in the war, our relationship can grow closer together. My Grandpa was a Marine back then, who fought for the Dutch (Indonesia was a Dutch Colony back then).

Q: What were you doing before you joined the military?

A: I was studying medicine at the University of Jakarta in Indonesia, before I was drafted into the Marines.

Q: What do you remember about your first days in the military?

A: I remember the rough time I had then. Boot Camp stood out the most because of the physical effort I had to put in.

Q: Where did you go during the war?

A: I traveled to Sulawesi ,which was formally called Celebes, Indonesia.

Q: What was your everyday life like?

A: I thought about my family back home a lot. I missed them. My living conditions were much different. I remember getting up really early and listening to role call. There was much physical exercises for us and we were mostly trained to be alert for an attack

Q: What was life like after war?

A: I was in peace, I was back home with my wife and I kept in shape. Mainly I was happy and at peace.

Student: Henry Ferguson
Civilian Interview: William Ferguson on his Uncle John Ferguson
Relationship to student: Great Uncle
Date and Location: by phone at my house, 3643 Hampstead Road, Los Angeles, 4/22/12
I chose this person because he was one of the only members of my family who actually served in the war. I had originally planned to interview my grandfather about his experience, as he was a poster child for the war effort. After speaking to him for a few minutes by phone I found out his uncle had actually served in the war and even earned a Purple Heart medal. I decided from there to change up the interview and ask him about his uncle instead. Proving to know a lot about what had happened I learned a lot about his Uncle and his experience. Here is the interview, unfortunately I was not able to record it.

Q. What did he do before he joined the military? Where did he live? Where did he attend school? Did he have a sweetheart?

A. He was living in Oil City Pennsylvania, had attended school at University of Wisconsin and played football as a student. He was also married to his wife Olive Jean. He was a bit of an outdoor man and enjoyed fishing in his spare time.

Q. Where did he go during the war?

A. He was in the Pacific campaign on Papa New Guinea. It was not good, the American troops were not trained to fight in jungles, the were being cut down by Japanese troops. As he progressed he was sent to Melbourne, Australia.

Q. What was he doing during the war?

A. During the war he was an officer, he started off as a 2nd lieutenant, then lieutenant, and then captain. At the time he was an infantry officer and was training them to fight in Melbourne, Australia. At this time he met General MacArthur and helped him train new recruits. He did see combat while he was on tour.

Q. Did he receive any medals or awards?

A. He received a Purple Heart, did not talk about how he got it. It is know in my fathers possession

Q. What was everyday life like for him?

A. He did not talk about anything that happened to him while on tour, beside what his wife knew he was very reclusive about it, he just wanted to forget. Did not want to have to remember what had happened while he was on tour. No letters where sent by him home either.

Q. What was life like after the war?

A. After the war he returned to his wife, he had three kids with her. He lived in Oil City until he had to move to New Mexico for cleaner air because one of his daughters had asthma. While in both Oil Cit and Albuquerque he established himself as a prominent businessperson. However, beside this success, he did suffer from what is know known as PTSD. He slept with a loaded gun under his pillow and never for more than six hours a night. He often went off on his own for hours on end by himself. His wife was very supportive about his condition. He was very quiet about his experiences and never talked about them. Many years later after he eventually opened up and began to tell stories to his wife and other family members, but there are many facts unknown.

Here are pictures of the Purple Hear he received

German Romero

Harold Hougland

No relationship to student

Interviewed 4/20/2012 at a senior center

Me: What were you doing before you joined the military?

Harold: I was attending Oakland City High School in Oakland City, Indiana before I was drafted.

Me: Were you drafted with any of your friends and at what age?

Harold: I was drafted when I was nineteen. I remember my best friend Lennis Gregory was also drafted with me and we decided to join the Navy.

Me: What did you do in the military?

Harold: I played the trombone in the band.

Me: What was your everyday life like?

Harold: I remember that being on land was very boring. While on the ship, I didn't write much, but I read a lot in the library. That's probably where I spent most of the time. The band guys and I liked to watch the planes arrive and depart from the ship. Sometimes we would play concerts for the soldiers as a form of entertainment.

Me: Where were you stationed?

Harold: First, I was stationed at Farragut, Idaho. Then, I was stationed at the USS Franklin. After that I was stationed at a Naval training camp in Ottumwa, Iowa.

Me: What are these pictures about?

Harold: Well, on March 19, 1945 at 7:07 a.m., our Aircraft Carrier, "USS Franklin," was operating with a task force sixty miles off the coast of Japan. Suddenly, two armor piercing 500 pound bombs hit us. One of the bombs fell among our fully armed and fueled planes which were intended for a strike on Kyushu, Japan. As these planes exploded, thousands of gallons of high octane aviation fuel were forced onto the hanger deck below the flight deck. That area became a blazing inferno, dooming hundreds of men to a fiery death. We spent a whole day fighting the fires, and since I was part of the band I also had the duty of being stretch bearer for the wounded or dead. Much more traumatic for me than the fear, however, was the task of burial at sea of 724 of my shipmates and the pitiful state of their bodies. Against all odds, our ship limped her way across the Pacific, through the Panama Canal and made it to the Port of New York; the most heavily damaged ship ever to reach home port under her own power. After all these years, I've never completely recovered from the effects of the horror of that fateful day, but I have learned to live with it and the nightmares no longer haunt me.

Harold and I

Damaged USS Franklin

Mass celebrated for the deceased

graduated. Retired Nov. 1, 1988. Then in March 2002 his wife passed. In 2004 he lost his ability to walk, but he still remains very independent. He still has friends from his time working at water and power (he mentioned that they are all women). Also, he still has a close relationship with wife's nephew.

Q: What did you do before the war?

Solid geometry (3-d Geometry which now is integrated into modern geometry class), calculus, and differential equations were the math (his favorite subject) courses at LA City College. Favorite sport is college football. He met Jessie Owens in college at a track meet. Mr. Braxton also ran as a sprinter until getting a ligament surgery in each leg. However, he can't recall what the condition was exactly.

> "It was rough, but it was worth it"
>
> --Eugene D. Braxton

Genarro Rogers
Eugene D. Braxton
Neighbor, Veteran, Friend

Greatest Google Generation

Q: Where were you born?

Born in Cincinnati, Ohio on Feb. 19, 1922. Moved to Los Angeles, CA in 1927. His dad passed 1934, his mom in 1965, his brother in 1960, and nephew in 1969. He said that these people meant a lot to him.

Q: Can you remember what you did when you found out Pearl Harbor was attacked?

He had just started working at Lockheed airfield 3 days before the attack on Pearl Harbor. On Dec. 7 1941 he said he was in church praying as he normally would. When he found out from a neighbor he and his friends didn't even know there was a Pearl Harbor. Then the next day the U.S. army arrived at the airfield, and they turned on radios for everyone and listened to Roosevelt declare war. The army started bringing women to do the men's jobs, therefore allowing more men to be drafted.

Q: Did you enlist in the army or were you drafted?

He was drafted into the navy January 1944. During physical exam, there were desks for each of the military branches. Blacks, however, were not allowed in the marines at the time. In his opinion though, the U.S. navy and Water and Power department were the two most racist organizations back then.

Q: Did you have any close friends that enlisted or were drafted?

He said he met some friends in the Navy, but hasn't really kept in touch. Other family of his include a brother --1 year older--, a nephew, a grand-nephew (principal of school and father of three) and grand-niece (member of LA Corrals and LA Opera company). He is also very proud that his son works for LA Times.

Q: What were you doing during the war? (i.e. jobs, assignments)

He first acted as an officer's servant. According to him, blacks were not trained to swim, and were not given formal combat training either. He was then sent to Washington before being sent to Pearl Harbor. Then he was assigned to the weather reporting ship U.S.S. Crystal (designated PY39). It was a large ship previously owned by a rich man, but since then had been repossessed and repurposed (fitted with guns, etc.) by the government. They stayed at sea for 40 days/ nights for each assessment. This made it much safer for the main army to travel the Pacific. They saw no combat. They did, however, see all of the Hawaiian Islands. They went back and forth from Pearl Harbor to resupply, and they stayed there for 20 days each time.

Q: What was your everyday life like?

At night he played checkers or cards. Daytime, however, officers kept them busy by making them cook, clean, and most other tasks on the ship.

Q: After the war was over, what did you do? How did you feel?

He said that he returned late October 1945. Sent to terminal island to be discharged December 1945. Some of his family came to welcome him back. In 1946 started working as postal service. Married in May 1950. Left the postal service in 1953. Worked then at department of water and power. He encountered racial discrimination when his promotion denied and given to a caucasian. However, one of his white friends helped him get it. The next promotion was being denied again by an even higher power. The department head kept transferring people into it so the position would never be open. Then a former city councilman helped him get that next promotion. Went back to college (USC was $11 per unit, and when he graduated it was $12 per unit) in 1951 under state GI bill to pursue scientific bachelors degree and in 1960 worked toward civil engineering by taking all night classes. His son was born in 1956. In 1973 he

Colin Owens

Gloria Demonteverde

Great-Great Aunt

Interviewed 4-25-12 over the phone

I chose to interview my great- great aunt because she was a teenager in the Philippine Islands when Japan first invaded. Although she was clearly not a soldier, she was in the middle of all of the conflict in that area and could provide firsthand recollections of the events there. Events such as her father, mother, and aunt almost being executed by a Japanese squad, only to be saved by her uncle. He could speak Japanese and he successfully convinced the soldiers to release the family. This is one of the many stories she told me during her interview.

Q: What was your everyday life like?

A: I was eleven when the war broke out. From the beginning of the invasion we were running from the Japanese soldiers. We had no idea where we were going to go next, we just went from refugee camp to refugee camp. We constantly had to hide for fear of being killed.

Q: What do you remember about the people in your community?

A: I remember being surrounded by family during this time. One time my father built a makeshift hut on a hillside so everyone could be together. We covered the top with big leaves to hide the smoke from the fire and we had to keep the dogs quiet, but it was fun.

Q: Do you remember how you felt about Japan before the war?

A: I remember how they sold product to us before the war. We thought they were friendly, but afterward we learned that they came to buy up all the scrap metal and stuff like that to prepare for war.

Q: Do you remember V-J Day?

A: Yes, there was a huge celebration, we all felt that we had won the war and we loved the American soldiers. We called them G.I. and we all felt that they had saved us.

Q: How did you get back into normal life, if ever, after the war?

A: We never really got back into normal life; all the schools were destroyed by the war. Most of the time we brought our own chairs and tables to school. One good thing was that the Americans stayed to help us rebuild and taught us how to speak English, which lead to my living here.

Austyn Bicarme
Veteran: Fred Baker
Relationship: Friend
Culver West Convalescent Hospital, 4.21.12

I was nervous upon entering this interview. Seeing Fred Baker, I thought that he was a very silent guy who didn't want to go too much into detail about his experience. I asked him if he had some time to discuss about his time around World War II for my history project. I read him the introduction of Mr. Line's *The Greatest Google Generation* Project and he found it amusing and chuckled at a couple of lines, including "Most if not all surviving members of the Greatest Generation couldn't tell you how to work an Ipad or how to text message". He laughed because he pointed out how true that statement is, even though he thinks it would be nice to own a nice phone or a high-tech tablet. He was very humble when he heard the term "Greatest Generation" and I felt the hospitality and friendliness of Mr. Baker. Our interview went for about 30 minutes and I have learned about what it was like for a teenager to experience things such as the Dust Bowl, the Great Depression, and WWII. After the interview, he was really pleased of the time I shared recounting his past. He even let me scan a photo of him when he was in the Marines. I would personally like to thank Mr. Baker for his huge contribution to our country and I think he most certainly receives the title of living in the "Greatest Generation".

1. What were you doing before you joined the military?
    a. Was around the age of 17 when WWII started.
    b. Attending high school
    c. Had a girlfriend who is now his wife
    d. Lived in Oklahoma
2. Do you remember how you felt about Japan or the war in Europe prior to Pearl Harbor?
    a. He was at a skating rink with his high school girlfriend, now his present day wife.
    b. When he heard the tragic event of Pearl Harbor he recalled how he felt affected by the devastation it brought to people who suffered. He kept those people in his prayers asking God for grace.
3. Did you enlist or were you drafted?
    a. Managed to hold a job for 18 months after the attack of Pearl Harbor.
    b. Due to peer influence, he decided to enroll in the Marines with a couple of his high school classmates.
    c. His mother was extremely nervous of the thought of her son going to war.
4. Where did you go during the war? What were some places you were stationed at?
    a. Put on a renovated freighter ship at places like Tahiti, the Samoan Islands, and Cook.
    b. Fred and his squad, at first, could not engage in combat because no one knew what to do.
    c. After they developed team work around 5 months of training, they did more island hopping from Munda to Bouganville and then to Milne Bay, around the time when he was a Private First Class
    d. In January, Fred was in the Philippines where he had duties including to hang bombs on S.B.D's and to synchronize machine guns.
    e. Was sent back to the U.S. to have his squad reformed.
        i. During this reformation, WWII ended and was discharged on November 1945.
5. What was you everyday life like?
    a. Truly missed the love of his life and it was even harder for him because he had just married her right before he was stationed at different places.
    b. Carried dear pictures of his family when he was young, and of course a picture of his wife Jennette.
    c. Everyone in his squad shared stories of home remembering old days in each of their high schools they came from.
        i. Also told stories of loved ones.
    d. Food was similar to what his high school cafeteria had: canned foods, especially canned beans, and also biscuits. There was not a lot of meat or vegetables because those would run out quickly

Michael Danon
Alfred Arthur Levin
Neighbor's Deceased Husband
Tuesday, April 24, 2012

Michael Danon: Do you remember how you and Arthur felt about the war in Japan and Europe prior to the Pearl Harbor bombing?

Genette Levin: We did not have any definite feelings about it. The whole country seemed to be in a very dramatic period.

MD: Do you remember how you felt the day Pearl Harbor was attacked?

GL: I do not vividly recall it. It was on a December day, but it was just an ordinary day. Then out of nowhere it just happened. I lived in Chicago at the time and found out about it immediately after it happened.

MD: Do you remember meeting any war heroes at the time?

GL: Well there was no real war heroes that I could recall because at that time we were just entering the war.

MD: Where was your husband stationed during the war?

GL: He was in the pacific campaign as a part of the Navy. He was in Japan for a short while, and he was on a fast troop carrier called the SS *Monterey*.

MD: Was your husband drafted or did he enlist?

GL: My husband knew he was going to be drafted, so he decided to enlist in the navy. He knew the Navy was a very clean and prideful group, and he was sickened by the idea of fighting trench wars. He also didn't want to be on the front lines.

MD: What was your husband's job in the Navy?

GL: He was in the Medical Core.

MD: Did he see a lot of combat?

GL: Fortunately, he did not. Although, the SS *Monterey* was chartered very close to a lot of deadly battles, so he saw his fair share of the war.

MD: Did your husband win any awards or medals?

GL: He didn't win anything for individual performance, but I recall all of the WWII vets being given some type of medal when they returned.

Alfred Arthur Levin
(to the left)

Thank you for your service to this country. May you rest in peace.

Joshua V. Dela Cruz
Civilian: Constancia T. Dela Cruz
Relationship: Grandmother
Date and Location of Interview: April 26, 2012 at my home

My grandmother is an incredible and important person in my life. When I was little and even now, she always takes care of me and tells me stories. Among these stories are stories of her childhood and the times during WWII. She would talk about how it was like being under the control of the Japanese and her experiences. She is the closest person to me who is from this generation and I would like to share her stories and experiences.

Q: Where did you live before Japan invaded the Philippines?
A: We lived in Mabalacat, Pampanga. It was no more than ten minutes away from the American Clark Air Base, which is the base that Japan bombed.

Q: What do you remember during the bombing of the Clark Air Base, or the invasion? How old were you?
A: I was nine years old and at home playing with friends and the family. Then we saw planes flying in the air. We didn't know what was happening. My parents and grandparents, told us to get inside and hide in the dugouts. It was an area we built and dug underground. There was a dug-out for each family. We stayed there overnight. The next day, our neighbor had a big truck and we got on it. They took us to the "barrio". In Philippines, a "barrio" is a small subdivision area, district, or neighborhood in cities or towns in Philippines. We went to the "barrio" Sapang Bayabas in Mabalacat; it is the closest to our house. We stayed there until the Japanese occupied the Clark Air Base. After that, we came back to our house. Japan was now occupying the Philippines.

Q: What do you remember from the Japanese Occupation? What changed? What happened?
A: It was very scary. Everyone was scared of the Japanese.
In the middle of the town, they had a sentinel. The sentinel was like a guard. When you pass by him, you have to bow. If you don't bow, they slap you. I remember my aunt passing by and she didn't bow, so they slapped her. I was scared to go pass by the sentinel. Everyone was scared.
In school, they taught the Japanese language. I still remember very few phrases.
Our parents and elders did not want us kids to be outside except to go to school. They were afraid of something happening to us.
I remember the Bataan Death March. American and Filipino soldiers were told to march from Bataan to Camp O'Donnell in Capas. They passed by our house in the streets. We were not allowed to give them food, talk, or interact with them, so we just watched.

Q: Do you know anyone who was in the Bataan Death March?
A. My first cousin was in the death march. He was in the army. When they were about reach Capas, somebody pulled him out and hid him in the house. The Japanese did not see him. When the soldiers finally left, the people, who saved him, let him go home. He lived in the "barrio" we go to. When he came home, his parents were in another "barrio", but we were there and very happy to see him. We fed him because he was very hungry.

Q: What do you remember about the end of the Japanese Occupation?
A: We went back to the "barrios" after seeing planes flying in the air. From another "barrio", people were shouting that MacArthur is back. When we heard the news, people were very happy. After a few days, we were able to go back home and the Japanese were gone. The Americans showed a film about the war. It was near Clark Field and everyone was invited. The film showed the time when the Americans left Philippines and when they came back. We were very happy to see the show and to be free from the Japanese.

Student: Jacob Kuljis
Veteran/ Civilian Interviewed: Cira Crisafulli
Relationship to Student: Grandmother
Date and Location of Interview: April 19, 2014 at the Crisafulli home

I chose to interview my Grandmother so I could learn more about her and my Grandfather's lives when they lived in Brooklyn, New York. All of my life my grandparents have told me stories of when they were younger and of when Grandpa was in the war. As I get older I would like to have some way of looking back on those stories and remembering my grandparents. This project is the perfect opportunity to record what their lives were like, and learn more about my family.

Q: What were you and Grandpa doing before he joined the military?
A: At that time we were living in Brooklyn, New York. I was working at Lord and Taylor's, a woman's department store and Grandpa was working at a pharmacy. We were engaged but not married yet.

Q: What do you remember about Grandpa's first days in the military.
A: Grandpa was training to be a pilot but when he did his solo flight test. The instructors said he was a little reckless, so he washed out. He than became an bombardier on the B-24s.

Q: What were you doing during the war? Any memorial experiences?
A: Grandpa was a bombardier on the B-24 bombers. One night, while on a mission, he jumped out of his plane. The impact gave him a blood clot in his leg and the blood clot kept him in the hospital for the next mission. On the mission grandpa was in the hospital , the plane was hit and everyone on it died except for the pilot. He was very lucky and it was an eye opening experience.

Q: What was Grandpa's everyday life like?
A: Grandpa would write home to me every day and I would write back. When he went on missions he couldn't send or receive letters or packages so some times he would get three or four at a time. His mother and I would sent him all kinds of food that he liked, spaghetti and meatballs, cookies, and Coca Cola in glass bottles. To send him the Coca Cola I had to wrap the bottles in cotton and newspaper, so they didn't break. His only reminder of home was a picture of me he kept in his locker.

Q: What do you remember about the other people in Grandpa's unit?
A: Grandpa became friends with another Italian boy. And one time after they came back from a mission, they had so many packages of food from home, between the two of them, that the took down a door in the barracks and used it as a stretcher to carry all the food. That night they had a party and fed every one in the barracks.

http://www.youtube.com/watch?v=Mj1HTrQ05fg

Student: Nick Leonard

Civilian Interviewed: Sole Surviving Son (Dad: Hal Thomas Leonard) on behalf of *Hal Thomas Gibson* **Relationship:** Grandfather **Date and Location of the Interview:** Wednesday, April 25, 2012 at students house.

Opening: I chose to interview my dad on behalf of my grandfather because he was my closest reference to finding out information about my grandfather and how he participated in WWII. I also think it is very interesting that my grandfather participated in the war. A few years ago, my dad told me that my grandfather participated in WWII and I never got around to asking him more about what my grandfather did. This project is the perfect opportunity for me to get to know more information about my grandfather in WWII.

1.) What were you doing before you joined the military?

Hal Thomas Gibson was living in Des Moines, Iowa. He attended Roosevelt High School and played many sports including football, boxing, basketball, and softball. He did have a sweetheart. His sweetheart was his wife.

2.) Did you enlist or were you drafted?

He was enlisted in the U. S. Marine Base of San Diego and inducted in the United States Marine Corps and Recruiting Station. He was 17 seventeen years old, almost turning eighteen, when he was enlisted in the military.

3.) Where did you go during the war?

He traveled to many different places. He was embarked aboard the U. S. S. Bataan on March 19, 1944 at San Diego and sailed until March 22 on that same year and arrived at Pearl Harbor. He also sailed on the U. S. S. LaSalle and arrived at Saipan, Marianas Islands. Another ship he went on was the U. S. S. Whitley at Hilo, Hawaii and arrived at Iwo Jima on February 19, 1945. He then sailed back to Hawaii from Iwo Jima on April 15, 1945.

4.) What was your everyday life like?

During the war, he worked as a rocket crewman and a rifleman. His job as a rocket crewman and rifleman were probably his most memorable experiences. He was imprisoned in Russia and questioned by the Soviet Union and possibly transferred.

5.) Were you awarded any medals or citations?

He was awarded a medal for the United Nations Service, National Defense Service, and for victory of World War II. He was also awarded many different later in his life in the Korean War, which includes the Purple Heart.
-The reason that there is not very much information (paperwork) is because some of it was

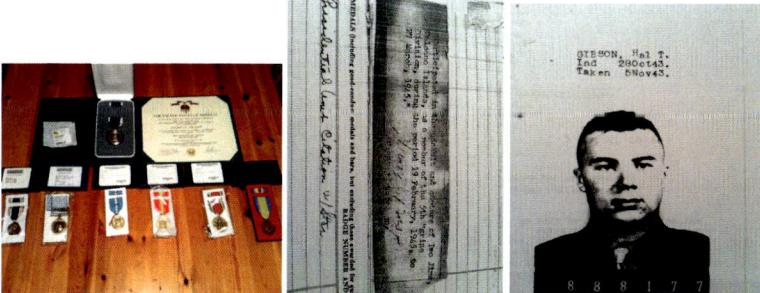

burned in a fire.

George explained how it was an exciting experience since he had never ventured outside of New Orleans before. He recalled his first time seeing an electric car and how he was cold, and how he had to get up at four in the morning. He said it was new, and it didn't bother him much.

Question #5/6: Where did you go during the war?
George didn't go far, mainly stayed in Maryland as an office boy; got to go to Washington and Chicago, and once to California. However, he said that his brothers were stationed in Chicago, Yorktown, Virginia, and in the Pacific as part of the Seamen Negro section. Evidently his brother Herbert was lucky enough to take up being a radioman, which was unusual for black man at the time.

Question #9: What was everyday life like?
George he wrote his current "sweetheart" Marie about his experiences. He told me how he and the fellow men had to eat nasty powdered eggs. He said he constantly felt home sick but carried no reminders or good luck charms.

Question #11: Did you come home on leave?
George said he came home after a couple months of basic service on leave in 1944. He said he came back to "back of town" in New Orleans because his mother wanted him home. He even drove a taxicab for some time.

Norey Smith

My Veteran: *George Smith Sr.*

Relationship: My great uncle on my father's side.

Date and Location of the Interview: Monday, April 23rd, 2012 in my living room.

Question #1: What were you doing before you joined the military?
George had been living in the predominately black Tremere Section of New Orleans called "back of town." He was in school doing a little part time work in the market delivering meat. He had "a few" girlfriends at the time; mainly stating he was still a young man at the time.

Question #3: Did you enlist or were you drafted?
George enlisted because it was the thing to do at the time; he followed in the footsteps of his two older brothers Ferdinand and Herbert. He enlisted by himself, no friends. The US Navy was the branch he chose, and he was then shipped to Maryland for boot camp. He said he had no true foresight as to what it would be like.

Question #4: What do you remember about your first days in the military?

Student: Peter Buese
Interviewee: Janet Buese
Relationship to student: Grandmother
Date of interview: 26 April 2012
Location: Over the phone

This interview is about my grandfather, Sherman, but since he is no longer alive, my grandmother answered questions about his life during WWII.

Q: Was he enlisted or drafted? Why did he choose his branch of service?

A: Sherm was drafted right before he finished college in 1940, although after his service he would eventually go back and finish his degree. Because of his background and his college major, he entered the Engineer Corp in the Army.

Q: What did he remember about his first days in the military? Did he do any advanced training?

A: He went through boot camp like any other person who was drafted or enlisted, but sometime afterwards he was either recommended or applied for the officer-training program. By the end of the war he was a Lieutenant Colonel.

Q: What was he doing during the war? What jobs or assignments did he have? Did he see combat?

A: He was an engineer, so he wasn't on the front lines of the war, but he does remember shooting his gun, although he never kept his head up long enough to see if he hit anything. His main specialty was to rehabilitate captured Japanese airfields on various islands in the Pacific, like Tinian. Since airfields were key in the Pacific, his job to fix up the airfields so that supplies and reinforcements could arrive was very important.

Q: What did he do to pass the time? Did he keep a journal or diary?

A: When he was not busy, he liked to play cards, write letters to friends and family, and write in his diary, which was unfortunately lost a long time ago.

Q: What was it like after the war? What were his first memories of going home? What work did he do?

A: After the war, he left the military for good, no reserve or anything. But when he got back to California, he picked up a job at Hawaiian Electric, moved to Hawaii with his first wife. She didn't like Hawaii for some particular reason, so they moved back to California, where Sherm finished his degree at USC, which was paid for by the GI Bill, and worked for California Edison for pretty much the rest of his life. The one thing I remember him telling me about the difference of home and the Pacific was the smell. He said that the stench of death on the Pacific Islands was unforgettable. Not only was it from dead soldiers, but farm animals were accidentally killed in the middle of the night, because soldiers would be so scared that they would shoot anything that did not say a password, assuming it was a Japanese soldier.

Student: Michael Reyes

Veteran / Civilian Interviewed: Val Reyes speaking on behalf of Valeriano Reyes

Relationship to the student: Father and Grandfather

Date and location of the interview: The Reyes house April 22, 2012

I have always known that my grandfather participated in World War 2; however, I never took the time to ask him about his time in the war, and so this project gave me the opportunity to spend the time to document my grandfather's war experiences. Unfortunately, my grandfather passed away, so I interviewed my father, who is also in the military, on behalf of my grandfather to recall some of the information.

Q: How did he get from being a part of the armed forces to being a part of the Bataan Death March?

A: At age 19 he volunteered to serve with a division of the army later that was later called the United States Armed Forces in the Far East. They fought the Japanese for three months until they surrendered on April 9, 1942. Valeriano along with fifty thousand Americans and Filipinos were forced to march for 9 days without food or water. Men who could not continue marching were executed.

Q: What was it like to have participated?

A: Many men were executed if they were unable to continue marching. To drink, they had to scoop muddy rainwater out of ditches along the road. Valeriano was also ordered to bury the dead. Even those that survived the march later died of malnutrition, malaria, and diphtheria.

Q: When did he eventually get out of the March?

A: On August 3, 1942, Valeriano pretended to be sick with malaria and he was freed to his sister who petitioned his release through the Red Cross. He was in the first group of prisoners released for medical help.

Q: After having gone through the death march, did he stop contributing to the army?

A: No, in 1944, he served in Markings Fill-Am Guerilla Dragon Intelligence unit and posed as an employee at the Mankayan mines to gather intelligence on the Japanese shipments of copper back to Japan. They captured and questioned him. They forced him to drink gallons of water hung him by his fingers and hit his body with a board. Bolo tribesman eventually helped him escape and he was honorably discharged in 1946 as a Master Sergeant.

Q: Has he received any recognition for participating in the Bataan Death March?

A: I actually applied to the Army Reserve Personnel Center in Missouri, but it was not until one year after I applied directly to Rep. Jane Harman for the medal to be presented. On October 5, 1997, I presented my father Valeriano Reyes, who was 73 at the time, with the World War 2 Prisoner of War Medal when I was still with my unit the 113th Medical Detachment Combat Stress Company.

Student: Ian Ross

Veteran/Civilian: Charles Ross

Relationship to the student: Grandfather

Date and location of interview: At my house with my father.

I choose to interview my dad about my grandfather for a few reasons. One was because I didn't know a lot about my grandfather because he died when I was five. Another was that I knew he was a cook so I wanted to know about non-combat troops in the war.

What were you doing before you joined the military?

I was going to high school and work odd jobs. I was actually applying for my citizenship at the time and they said I could get it by joining the armed forces.

Where were you living?

I was living in a suburb outside Detroit after I emigrated from Scotland.

Did you have a sweetheart?

I didn't have a sweetheart but I married the love of my life when I got out of the military.

Did you enlist or were you drafted?

I was offered a quicker way of getting my citizenship and I viewed it as a chance to serve my future home country.

What did you envision it would be like after you joined?

I wanted to be a cook because I had experience in the kitchen and I felt that was a good way to help the troops without having to kill someone.

What do you remember about your first days in the military?

I remember doing basic training and getting assigned to the Pacific fleet as a cook.

What were you doing during the war?

I was stationed on a couple different battleships and aircraft carriers in the Pacific. I would wake up everyday and make hundreds of scrambled eggs and bacon for all the troops. My everyday experiences ranged from cooking to organizing storerooms within the ships. My living conditions were separate from the barracks of the other sailors so they were a step up.

What was it like after the war?

I got home and I worked on a golf course and started a family with my new wife.

What did you do? How did your career develop after that?

After that I became a salesman for large tractors and machinery, and I eventually went on to own several golf courses.

Thomas Steinke
Donald Engh
Family Friend
April 14, 2012

I chose to interview Mr. Engh because he has told me some incredible stories in the past and I would like to share them with you. He was on many missions as a B-25 bomber pilot in the Pacific. You would not think him to be in constant danger like the ground troops, but he was always in fear for his life as a highly valuable target to the Japanese when in the air and on the ground.

Q: Where did you go during the war?
A: During the war Don was stationed on the island of Okinawa. When he got there the climate was drastically different. There was never a time when it wasn't humid and hot. He also remembered while being there that there was nothing cold to drink, everything was warm and unpleasing.

Q: What were you doing during the war?
A: Don was a Lieutenant at the age of nineteen commanding the medium bomber. When he was not flying, Don was a photography officer and was in the intelligence branch as well. One of his most memorable experiences was when he got a radio call to abandon his bomb load and fly back to base, little did he know, that the Atomic Bomb was about to be dropped. After the bomb went off, he flew to the drop sight with his crew and was stunned and terrified by the destruction.

Q: What was your everyday life like?
A: Don passed the time on Okinawa by writing letters to his girlfriend back in the United States, and doing math problems to keep from getting bored. He remembers that he was home sick because he missed going to the local diner with his friends and having fun. Out of everything, Don craved a nice malt to cool him down while in the humid Pacific.

Q: Do you remember V-E Day and V-J Day when the war ended?
A: Mr.Engh remembers the end of the war very vividly. He said that the sky over the island was completely lit up. He was scared as well as being happy because the whole island was shooting all their firearms or artillery in the air. At the time, it was a great idea but when the bullets and shells came down it was simply terrifying. After the war ended he stayed just over six months. To him the end of the war meant a new start.

Q: What was it like after the war?
A: When Donald came home he said it felt like a big void in time. He missed so many things, but he believed it was more important to serve his country. The first thing he wanted to do was buy a car, but because of the war efforts, the manufacturing of cars was scarce. Don was lucky because he found a 1937 Ford convertible that he paid a thousand dollars for. After getting back to California, he took advantage of the G.I. bill and went to USC for his education. When he finished with school he settled down and started a family.

Joshua Mora
Veteran Interviewed: Paul Rancour
Interview conducted on April 22

Although none of my family members were directly involved with World War 2, I found a wealth of information through an interview via email with Mr. Paul Rancour. His experiences in the Navy during the Second World War showed his true dedication towards protecting the country that he loved dearly. His stories, along with the stories of his peers, should be shared and shared again, for we can learn so much.

Paul Rancour grew up in Lakewood, Ohio and lived there until he was 24. With Paul being her only son, Paul's mother was upset when Paul decided to join the Navy. Going against his mother's wishes, Paul was determined to serve his country and in December of 1941, he joined the Navy. "I joined the Navy to help defend my country, and my freedom." Paul first enlisted in the Navy in Cleveland, Ohio. After that, Paul traveled to the Western United States where he underwent extensive training for eighteen months. After his training, Paul worked as a mechanic on the USS Essex. Paul first boarded the USS Essex in 1943, and was eventually stationed in the South Pacific Ocean. His first mission was the raid on Marcus, which was only about 1000 miles from Japan. It was hit once before by American troops and another attack was a complete surprise. Japanese planes were attacked and destroyed. Air Group Nine, the group that Paul belonged to, was battle-tested.

      The Essex was involved in many battles throughout the war. Major battles that involved the Essex were the attack on Wake Island, the raid of Kwajalein, the raid on Rabaul, the Battle of the Marshalles, and the raid on Truk Island. These battles occurred between 1943 and 1944, and the Essex was almost always victorious. The only attack against the Essex was through a Kamikaze. No one died during the attack, except for the pilot of the plane. When the war was coming to an end, Paul returned to his home in Cleveland, Ohio.

Student: Nathan Blais

Veteran Interviewed: Ray Molina

Relationship to Student: Found through the Redondo Beach Veteran's Center

Date and Location of the Interview: April 20, 2012 Redondo Beach, California

I chose to interview Mr. Molina due to the fact that I don't have family members currently alive who served in World War II. I found him by calling the Redondo Beach Veteran's Center who then directed me to him. Mr. Molina was originally from Houston, TX and had served in the Navy in both World War II and the Korean War on the USS Walke. When he returned home he became an artist and met Hubert Humphrey, Ronald Reagan, and Gene Autry.

1. What were you doing before you joined the military?
    a. He grew up in Houston, Texas and was attending high school when he joined the war effort. Everyone at the time had a high school sweetheart. He never revealed if he had one before he left for the war.
2. Do you remember how you felt about Japan or the war in Europe prior to Pearl Harbor?
    a. He said the Japanese "were the meanest creatures in the world" after learning of Pearl Harbor, but no ill thoughts of the Japanese before it.
3. Did you enlist or were you drafted?
    a. He had enlisted after they started drafting people because he felt obligated to do his duty as a citizen and those who enlisted had better options then those drafted. He said that he "lucked out" and was selected for the Navy, which according to Mr. Molina was better because he did not die in the war, while his friend who was selected for the army, did.
4. What do you remember about your first days in the military?
    a. He remembered that his boot camp training took place in San Diego and that was a very enjoyable experience. He recalled one of his training sergeants, Sergeant Sweeny, who would punish people who goofed off by making them hold their gun over their head and run around the exercise field and scream "I am an Asshole!" for an hour.
5. What was your everyday life like?
    a. Mr. Molina's life on the ship was not bad by any means. Everyone on the ship wrote letters home to his own family. He said that crewmembers were assigned to read the mail that was to be sent out. The mail was censored to prevent sensitive information such as locations of ships and move orders from being intercepted or leaked to the enemy. The most common things people ate on the ship were pork and beans. The living conditions on the ship were cramped, but sanitary. He slept on a hammock in a large room filled with other crewmembers. When I had asked him about his friend on the ship, he became very emotional and it was hard for him to answer the questions.

Student: Kerrigan Madden
Veteran interviewed: Gene Pohl
Relationship: Grandfather
Date and location of interview:
    West Covina, California. April 26, 2012

I interviewed my grandpa because he is the
member of the Greatest Generation whom I know
the best. He had talked about serving in the
military during World War II, and I wanted to find
out more about his experience.

Question: What were you doing before the military?
Answer: Before joining the military, I was in high school. I lived at home in San Diego, CA. When Pearl
Harbor was bombed, I was 13 (I turned 14 the following week). I remember that day very well. I was 17
when I enlisted. I had a sweetheart in high school, but not when I enlisted.

Question: What do you remember about your first days in the military?
Answer: I took the train to basic training in Wichita Falls, Texas at Shepherd Field, and I remember it being a
long trip. The first days of the military I remember inoculations and written tests. In basic training, I learned
how to march and how to fire weapons – an M 16 rifle, a 45 caliber pistol and 45 caliber machine gun. We had
many drills on marching and weapons training. We woke up early every morning and marched to breakfast.
There was a lot of outdoor field training.

Question: What do you remember about other people in your unit?
Answer: I had a close friend named Frank Reis from Santa Maria, CA. We had no casualties in our unit.

Question: What was your everyday life like?
Answer: We lived in barracks, which had two different platoons, with 30 men on each floor.
I was apprehensive, but not scared during the first days of basic training.   I had 12 weeks of basic training. The
final training consisted of a 20 mile hike, where we camped out and slept on the ground for several days. I
occasionally felt homesick. After basic training, I went to advanced training at a message center operator
school in Scottsdale, Illinois, for 4 weeks.

Question: Did you come home on leave?
Answer: I went home on leave to visit my parents and see old friends. My first leave was Christmas, for 7 days. I
also got a 10 day pass after my 2nd training and before I went to Hickam Field in Hawaii for my 18- month
enlistment.

Alex Acosta
Victor J. Subia
Friend of Grandma
April 21, 2012 at Mr. Subia's house
I chose to interview Mr. Subia because I am first generation Mexican-American. Since my grandparents were not in the United States during World War II, I had to ask my Grandma if she had any friends that served in World War II. My Grandma, fortunately, had a friend named Mr. Subia, and she was able to introduce me to him.
1. Did you enlist or were you drafted?

The United States Army drafted Mr. Subia at the age of 25 in 1942. He says he had a strong feeling of nationalism because the year before he was drafted, Pearl Harbor was attacked. Mr. Subia had a copy of the Azusa Herald from 1942. The Azusa Herald had an article that called for 20 residents in the Azusa area to report for training.
2. What do you remember about your first days in the military?

Mr. Subia had to report to Camp Fannin Texas for basic training. The basic training consisted of rifle and communication training. After his seven weeks of training was finished, he had to report to Fort Ord to receive his oversea assignment. On his way overseas, the 99th Signal Battalion and Mr. Subia stopped to see the remains of Pearl Harbor and strengthen their national pride.
3. What were you doing during the war?

Mr. Subia was ranked Technician 5th Grade. His role in the war was to set up radio message centers and wire the communications. Mr. Subia recalls landing on Los Negros Island in the Admiralty Islands campaign. He spent several days in foxholes when the Japanese were attacking. He remembered that 3,005 men were killed, only 98 being American.
4. What was your everyday life like?

Mr. Subia tried writing letters to his family and wife every other day because he was often homesick. He would not know if she received his letters. He had to eat canned food everyday and on a good day, he would eat eggs. He remembers the living conditions being muddy and rainy. While at sea, he recalls many waterspouts getting very close to his ship.
5. Do you remember V-J Day when the war ended?

Mr. Subia vividly remembers V-J Day but was sent to Hiroshima as an occupation soldier. He remembers the hostile stares from the Japanese, no buildings standing, corpses on the ground, and the stench of death. Mr. Subia iterated that he would never forget the images from the bombing of Hiroshima. Mr. Subia's job in Hiroshima was to help with the maintenance work of rebuilding. He was assigned this job because he could speak Japanese and had experience with maintenance.

Alejandro Aguila
Veteran: Hank Hinman
Relationship: Friend of a Friend
Interviewed at Hank Hinman's house in Whittier, CA
April 22nd 2012.

I chose to interview Hank Hinman, for I believe his story is worth to be heard. He was a man who stood up for he is country when it needed him, and still to this day, he takes pride in answering the call. He was not your average naval officer on deck; Hank Hinman experienced the war and its full effect.

1. **Did you enlist or were you drafted?**
   a. "I enlisted of course, even though I did not really understand what war was truly about. I was only 19, but the majority of my friend enlisted, so I felt that I had to do my part for the country. I first enlisted at our neighborhood pool, but they didn't want to take me because I had flat feet, so I went to Millington Tennessee to enroll myself in the Navy, and they took me without any question."

2. **Where did you go during the war?**
   a. "I was stationed on the USS Makin Island of in the ocean near Iowa Jima. The first time I left Kansas was when I was sent to boot-camp, and I had no difficulty adjusting there, but when I was stationed on the Makin Island, it was a shock. I have never been to the ocean, let alone live on it. It was all a complete different experience on its own."

3. **What was your everyday like?**
   a. "You really didn't have an average day, you were always occupied with different tasks here and there, but for one thing, there were always tensions arising. Sometimes it took weeks to get letters back from family and loved ones, and when we did get letters, many of them were 'Dear John' letters. To pass time we laid on the deck of the ship and took in some sun or went below deck to get ice-cream."

4. **What where you doing during the War?**
   a. "I was assigned in charge of the communication and the 15 cal gun on a TBF-6 plane. We constantly went on missions, and I was also a part of the 3 day bombing of Iwo Jima, but none of those missions can compare to the one when our plane was hit and had to make a crash landing on the primitive island of New Guinea. I was barely getting use to being in the sky; nothing could have prepared me for being shot out of the sky. We were stranded for over 4 days on the island until rescue came, and boy what a hectic four days those were..."

5. **Were you awarded any medals or citations ?**
   a. Yes I was awarded quite a medals. I received metals usually on every mission that we went on, but my more recognized metals were my 18 air medals and 4 distinguished flying medals over the period of November 43'-July'45.

Student: Ignacio Galicia
Veteran/Civilian Interviewed: Richard Trujillo through his son David Trujillo
Relationship to the student: My dad's friend's friend
Date and location of the interview: April 25, 2012 at David Trujillo's house
Opening. Why you chose to interview your Veteran/Civilian. A short introduction paragraph: My parents had invited their friends over and my dad's friend happened to know someone that I could interview, thus I made arrangements to interview that person.

1. What were you doing before you joined the military? He worked as a construction carpenter.
   Where were you living? Douglas, Arizona
   Where did you attend school at the time? He did not remember.
   Did you have a sweetheart? No
3. Did you enlist or were you drafted? He enlisted at the age of 17
   What motivated you to enlist? The ability to being able to serve this country while also exploring different parts of the world motivated him to enlist.
   Did any friends enlist with you? No, but a group of his cousins came together to enlist with him.
   Where did you go to join? He went to Phoenix, Arizona to be processed into the navy.
   Why did you choose your branch of service? Although Richard wanted to serve in a different branch of service, he and his cousins were needed men to be placed in the navy.
   What did you envision it would be like after you joined?
   He envisioned that he would be relatively safer than on land because he was on a ship and that he would not be led into so much fire from enemies.
5. Where did you go during the war? He toured through the islands of the pacific, islands of the Phillipines, Leyte, Samar, Manus, Pearl Harbor, and was present in the battle of Iwo Jima.
   Where were you stationed first? He did not remember the exact island, but it was one of the islands of the pacific.
   Do you remember when you first arrived at the new location? (How did you feel?) He did not have so many feelings about that because he was told before-hand that the boat he was on served as a transport vessel. So because it served as a transport vessel it was constantly arriving at new ports, David's father never obtained a hearty array of feelings.
   Did you travel to other places?
   Yes, he traveled to parts of the Philippines, Samar, Leyte, Luzon, and Manus.
6. What were you doing during the war? He served as a gunner on the USS Cape Johnson vessel.
7. What jobs or assignments did you have? He served in the Pacific theater and was a gunner on the USS Cape Johnson vessel.
   Did you see combat? Yes he did see combat because the ship he was on was being shot at.
   Can you tell me about your most memorable experiences?
   His most memorable experience was hearing word that after being bombard by enemy fire during a fight around Christmas 1944 that lasted from December 28 to January 7. Not a single strike was landed on the ship.

9. What was your everyday life like? He would hear constant complains from other shipmates who wanted more action then just staying in the boat. There was always plenty of food and supplies on the ship. During some days, the ship would get very stuffy and hot inside.
   Did you write many letters home? Did people write to you? What did you want to say? Yes he did write and receive many letters home to his sister and mother. He mainly wanted to know descriptively what they were doing at that time or how things were running at home. In this way, he would picture himself as being there with them and forget that he was at war.
   What was food like? Did you always have enough food?
Because he lived on board, there were always plenty of rations, except when they would transport a group of soldiers. He said that food was in variety on the ship, so food for him was good.
   How were your other supplies and equipment?
Supplies and equipment were usually always well organized and labeled mainly because they needed to constantly tend to the soldiers that came abroad.
   What were your living conditions like?
On the ship, things were usually well kept and comfortable enough to sleep tight when soldiers were not on board. When soldiers were on board, it was often too stuffy and hot to sleep/rest comfortable.
   Were there times when you felt homesick or stressed? Yes there were times he felt stressed, especially when bombs and gunfire could be heard at night. The stress that one of those strikes could hit the ship at any moment was terrifying. Anytime he would receive or right back to his sister and mother, he would feel homesick. If he saw other shipmates passionately looking at pictures of their children or wife, he would always feel a little homesick.
   Did you carry any reminders of home with you?
He kept letters and pictures from his aunts, sisters, and mother.
   Did you believe in any "good luck charms" or superstitions?
He wore a metal that he wore through service and also carried his dog tags.

until I was married, at the age of 24 in 1952. I was trained as a teacher and taught Science at La Puente High School, then became the principal of Los Altos High school in 1960. I retired as the Deputy Superintendent of Schools in the Hacienda La Puente Unified School District in 1986.

Student: Jonathan Robert Dezzutti
Veteran/Civilian Interviewed: Geno Ario Dezzutti
Relationship: Grandfather
Date & Location of Interview: April 22, 2012 in West Covina, California

Opening: My relationship with my grandfather, Geno Ario Dezzutti, has been strong ever since I can remember. When this project was assigned, I viewed it as an opportunity for my relationship with my grandfather to grow. To be honest, I had no clue that my grandfather was in the service around World War II and am very pleased to now have these interview responses in my possession.

Q: What were you doing before you joined the military?
A: I was finishing up my freshman year at U.S.C. after graduating from Cathedral High School in June of 1945. World War II had just ended, but I was still subject to the World War II Draft. At the time, I had wanted to join the navy; however, my folks would not sign the enlistment papers because they were opposed to militarism. Consequently, I was drafted in April of 1946, after I had turned 18 on Dec. 31, 1945. At the time I was drafted, I was living at home with my mother and father in the Highland Park area of Los Angeles. I did not have a permanent sweetheart, but I was dating a girl form U.S.C. as well as a girl I had met in high school.

Q: Did you enlist or were you drafted?
A: I wanted to enlist in the navy because that was the favored branch of the service amongst my friends, but my folks were against it, and you needed your parents signed permission to enlist if you were under the age of 18. So, by the time I had turned 18, I had no choice, and was drafted into the army. Several of my friends from high school were older than me and their folks were willing to sign the papers, so off they went to the navy. As it turned out, my experiences in the army were fascinating, and I never regretted not being able to join the navy. It's important to know that patriotism during World War II was much different than what it is today. Young men of my generation wanted to serve their country! I had never been out of southern California when I went into the army, and I did not have the faintest idea of what it was going to be like or where I would be going.

Q: Where did you go during the War?
A: After my induction into the army at Camp Beale in the Sacramento area of northern California, I was sent on a troop train through the southern part of Arizona and New Mexico to Fort Bliss, Texas. I had no say in where I was going or what I would be trained to do. As it turned out, Fort Bliss was an anti-aircraft training base and I had spent 2 months in July and August of 1945 training to be an anti-aircraft gunner. After basic training, I went home on leave for a couple of weeks, and was then sent to Camp Stoneman in the San Francisco bay area waiting to be shipped overseas. When my buddies and I read the orders that we were going to be shipped to Korea, we were astounded – we had never heard of Korea and had no idea where it was located or what it was like! I served in Seoul. Pusan, Kwanju, Taegu, Chinju, and Irie.

Q: What was your everyday life like?
A: When I arrived in Seoul, Korea, after 14 days at sea crossing the Pacific Ocean, the whole scene was so strange and surreal to an 18 year old who had never been out of California! The smells, sounds, looks of the towns, and even the looks of the people were so different from any thing I had ever known or seen! Because I had one year of college before I was inducted, I was asked if I would be interested in police work, and I thought, "why not – at least Military Police were well fed, and decently dressed " – so I said, :"Yes." Lucky me, I was chosen to train to be an agent in the Army's Criminal Division, investigating major crimes committed by or against U.S. Military personnel. It was a marvelous experience in every way and I truly loved it! I worked on cases involving assault, arson, murder, fraud – you name it! I really never felt homesick or lonely due to the fact that I was too busy in fascinating work. We C.I.D. agents lived in our own private homes within Korean cities, far removed from other military personnel. The food was very good and we did not lack for anything, including supplies and equipment. I didn't carry any specific reminders of home with me, but it remained in the back of my head. While there, I did not believe in any "good luck charms" or superstitions.

Q: What was it like after the war?
A: Even though my time in the army was exciting and a real adventure, I was ready to come home. After 18 months in the army, I was discharged and came home to my folks in 1947. I immediately returned to U.S.C., and graduated with a Bachelor's degree in 1950. I followed that up with a Master's degree in 1951. I lived at home with my parents

Student: Martin Kim
Veteran/Civilian Interviewed: Man Gyu Kim
Relationship to the student: Grandfather
Date and Location of the interview: April 23rd, 2012 over e-mail and phone

My grandfather, Man Gyu Kim, was 10 years old at the time World War II began. Japan took control of Korea and many soldiers were in the country at the time. My grandfather remembers a few details about the war and about the Japanese soldiers in his hometown of Hwanghaedo, North Korea. As he goes on with the interview, my grandfather expresses his feelings and the memories of his childhood when the times weren't so great,

1) **Q**: How did you feel about Japan's taking over Korea and what do you remember seeing as a child?
   A: As a child, I remember my country's people feeling very frustrated. Korean was a weaker country than Japan so we had no choice but to be taken over. It was very frustrating to the point of tears. I remember seeing many soldiers in my hometown.

2) **Q**: Did you see any Japanese soldiers during World War II and how did you feel about seeing the soldiers?
   A: Yes, I saw soldiers during my childhood. I was in 5th grade attending elementary school. Because of my age, I did not feel any anger or fury but rather, I felt that they were very cool and they also looked gentle.

3) **Q**: During the war, were any family members or relatives drafted to the army to fight?
   A: No, none of my family members or relatives were drafted to the army.

4) **Q**: What were you doing at the time of the war?
   A: During the war, I was attending elementary school and just like any other student, I was keeping up with my grades and working hard.

5) **Q**: What did you think of the war?
   A: At the time of the war, I thought that Japan would turn out to be the winner of the war because Japan was much stronger than Korea.
   > **Q**: At the time of the war, were you mad, sad, or scared?
   > **A**: No, I wasn't angry, sad, or mad. The Japanese soldiers told me that when I grew up, I would have to join the army so I thought that when I grew up I would have to join the Japanese army.

6) **Q**: How did you feel after the war?
   A: After the war, since all the Japanese soldiers left, I felt elated and my country was relieved to see all Japanese forces out.

7) **Q**: Did the Japanese soldiers mistreat or do anything wrong?
   A: Although the Japanese soldiers did nothing to me, I have seen the soldiers beat the Korean people and take what wasn't theirs. I saw some innocent people killed. The Korean people did nothing to them but their lives were still taken.

My grandfather and grandmother

Student: Vincent Andrew Lopez
Veteran Interviewed: Harold LaForce
Date of the interview: April 18th, 2012.
Location: Home of Harold LaForce.
Relationship: Neighbor

Harold LaForce has been a dear friend and neighbor of my family ever since we moved to West Covina. He's constantly willing to help out with anything we need. His persistence to push on in life is very inspiring, and because of this I felt Harold should be known by others. I found out a while ago that he was apart of World War II, and when this project was given to me I knew Harold would be perfect for interviewing. This was our interview:

Q's1: **What were you doing before the war? Were you attending school? Did you have a sweetheart?**
A: *I lived on a farm in Oskaloosa, Iowa. I attended a country school where the years were from 1-8. I didn't have a sweetheart, not really. Too bashful.*

Q's2: **Do you remember how you felt about Japan or the war in Europe prior to Pearl Harbor? Do you remember the day Pearl Harbor was attacked? Were you able to meet famous war heroes of the time?**
A: *I don't remember I felt about all that prior to Pearl Harbor. But yes, I do remember the day Pearl Harbor was attacked. And no, I don't think I met any of them.*

Q's3: **Where did you go during the war? Where were you stationed? How was the trip there? How did you feel when you arrived at the new location? Did you travel to other places?**
A: *I went to the Pacific Islands. I think I was stationed at the Island of Morotai. I remembered the trip there, you better believe it, 10,000 on the ship. It was murder... no, it wasn't murder. I can't say that, we're interviewing. They had troughs in there and people threw up in them. Luckily, I didn't get seasick. I don't remember how I felt when I arrived at the new location. I traveled to other Islands.*

Q's4: **What did you do during the war? What was your most memorable experience?**
A: *I was a file clerk in an office. My most memorable experience was.. I guess the Jap's flying over and we dove in a foxhole, I believe.*

Q's5: **What was your everyday life like? Did you write many letters home? What did you want to say? What was the food like? Did you always have enough food? How were your other supplies and equipment? What were your living conditions like? Were there times when you felt homesick or stressed? Did you carry any reminders of home with you? Did you have a good luck charm?**
A's: *Pretty routine, just served on KP and spent eight hours in an office where the Captain and the Lieutenant worked under a Sergeant or Major. I wrote quite a few letters to my family and one girlfriend. The letters were restricted and went under a sensor, so not much could be said. The food was terrible. We ate Australian sheep, with more than enough for everybody. It wasn't lamb, it was ogre sheep. Other than that, we were supplied very good. However, the islands were hot and we slept with a net to keep the mosquitos off of us. I didn't feel homesick because I was surrounded by lots of people. My dad died while I was over there. I didn't have a good luck charm.*

Video of interview: **http://www.youtube.com/watch?v=GO0F1kuNAGA**

Jacques Spinner

Paul Spinner

Grandfather (dad side)

Home (back deck), April 8, 2012

The Greatest Google Generation: Paul Spinner

I chose to interview my grandfather because he is the very close to me and is a living World War II Veteran. He grew up in West Wood and lived at 3659 West 59th place for one year. He then moved after his mother divorced his father. He grew up with no true father figure so he was very attached to his mother. He remembers her calling him her "little man". He is currently 89 years old and still strong, according to his doctor. My grandfather served in the navy for four years.

#3 Did you enlist or were you drafted? Paul Spinner volunteered and enlisted into the navy at age 23. His motivation came from the Japanese attack on the South Pacific and China. He didn't enlist with any friends. He joined at the Naval ROTC at UCLA.

#6 What were you doing during the war? He was on board a Naval Destroyer called the Stockham "DD683" along with 49 other destroyers who were anti submarine ships that protected Air Craft Carriers. He was on picket duty a lot which is like boat cleaning and making sure all the equipment is working. When they were attacking they would be doing shore bombardment.

#7 What do you remember about the other people in your unit? Officer O'Neil was the only man he saw get hurt, he lost an eye due to a gunshot wound. The bullet got lodged in his skull.

#9 What was your everyday life like? He had two four hour duty shifts and also had to check the ships anti air guns which was a first lieutenants job. Officers ate in the Ward Room, served by African Americans. He was very well fed three times a day. He had a private cabin with room service. He didn't carry any charms but kept a picture of his mother in his wallet.

 # 10 What did you do to pass the time? He would sit and read and on occasion be able to have some wine. He didn't really keep a diary but would jot down important tasks or things he had to get done in upcoming days. Every day was very professional and serious.

YouTube Link - http://youtu.be/Wfi2SPnGttE

A: For him, at least, there was always enough food because he was the Captain's Cook. He mentioned it being high quality because of that and having state-of-the-art equipment.

Q: What were his living conditions like?

A: Kind of crammed... there were about two or three bunks on top of each other and several to a room.

Q: Did Uncle A.J. Carry any reminders of home with him?

A: He usually had a few photo albums with pictures of family and friends to keep his morale up

Student: Cameron Walker

Veteran/Civilian Interviewed: Lynette Broussard-Walker about Arthur James Copper

Relationship (of veteran) to student: Great Uncle

Relationship (of interviewee) to student: Mother

Relationship of interviewee to veteran: Niece

Date and location of the interview: 23 April 2012, my house, Los Angeles, CA

For this interview my ideal veteran would have been my uncle, Arthur James "A.J." Copper. He was in the Navy during the late 1930s until the mid-1940s. He worked as a Captain's Chef and spent most of his memorable time travelling the world. My uncle, A.J., was on the U.S.S. Tennessee the day of the bombing at Pearl Harbor. Since he is no longer living, I decided to interview my mother, his niece, instead.

1. Q: What was Uncle A.J. doing before he joined the military?
    A: He was living in Franklin, LA going to school at Franklin High School.
2. Q: Did he enlist or was he drafted?
    A: Your uncle enlisted on October 7, 1939.
    Q: What motivated him to enlist?
    A: He just wanted to leave Franklin. His cousin made the Navy look glamorous and A.J. just wanted to see the world outside of where he had been his whole life.
    Q: Did any of his friends enlist with him?
    A: No.
    Q: Where did Uncle A.J. have to go to enlist?
    A: The station in New Orleans.
    Q: Why did he choose his branch of service?
    A: Like I said, his cousin made it seem like the ideal lifestyle to be living and he wanted to get away from home.
    Q: What did he envision it would be like after he joined?
    A: Perfect. He thought seeing the world and being on the open ocean would be amazing.
3. Q: Where was Uncle stationed first?
    A: Pearl Harbor. He was very excited, too.
    Q: Did he go anywhere else before or after the war?
    A: Yes. He travelled to a few islands in the South Pacific: the Philippines, Fiji… places like that.
4. Q: What jobs or assignments did Uncle A.J. have?
    A: Due to segregation, blacks couldn't really get high-ranked positions, but he was the highest rank available to him at the time: the Captain's Cook.
    Q: Did he see combat?
    A: Yes; he was on the Destroyer a few times when the Navy was fighting out at sea.
    Q: What was his most memorable experience?
    A: Definitely being on the U.S.S. Tennessee when it got bombed on December 7th, 1941.
5. What was his everyday life?
    Q: Did he send home many letters to his family and/or friends?
    A: Not really. The whole point of him joining the Navy was to get away from home.
    Q: What was the food like and was there always enough?

PACIFIC THEATRE

Dec. 7th 1941 a day that will live in infamy! This day pulled thousands of Americans into WWII. The Pacific War saw the **Allied powers** pitted against the Empire of Japan. The United States and Japan endured four hard years of war in the Pacific that finally saw an end in 1945.

These are the stories from those who were there..

Q: Who were his main friends and comrades that he met in camps/training or in his fleet? Were there any casualties of his friends?

A: His close friends were Benjamin O. Davis, Max Robinson, and Jimmy Walker and the rest of the members in his unit that I can't remember exactly. Dudley Watson was an officer, but during his time in the air force, there was prejudice, so there was much tension between the white and the black members of the army. Jimmy Walker was one casualty in his unit, for he was shot down. The Tuskegee Airmen didn't have any casualties in the war, for the only time where these men died was after the war.

Q: Did he ever write letters to you? Did he have any complaints about the food or supplies? Also was he very homesick?

A: I wrote letters to him every single week. I talked about both of our families, what I was doing, what new people I'd met, and letters about everyday life. He wrote about day-to-day situations, not much about combat. He wrote about things in the air force bases in Germany, but he did not write much about the combat in the war. He never complained about how the food was like in the air force bases. I am not good cook, and my husband didn't complain about the taste of my food as long as he ate something. I remember he said that all supplies or equipment that he needed for his duties, the air force would give it to him. If he needed some repairs in the planes, the air force commanders would supply. There were times where he felt homesick. He always wrote letters to me every week to see how everyone at home was doing. He was not superstitious and didn't really carry any "good luck charms", but he was very serious in his duties. He just did what he needed to do, and he succeeded in his roles.

I will never forget, on January 20th, 1958, he had to fly 4 hours every night to stay on "flying pay." He flew at 6:00 p.m. to 10:00 p.m. for readiness (in case of attacks). This night, he died in a plane accident around 9:00 p.m. At 12:00 midnight, the Chaplin and my husband's friend Benjamin O. Davis and his wife came to tell me that my husband has passed away. Dudley was flying as a copilot and the main pilot, Mr. Richardson, had difficulties with the plane. They almost made the landing, but the plane unfortunately exploded.

Matthew Young
Mrs. Bernice Watson
My Cousin's Grandmother
April 22, 2012. San Pedro, California

I chose to interview Mrs. Bernice Watson because I knew she has a great memory on the memories with her and her deceased husband. I thought it would be a great opportunity for me to gain more knowledge of the Tuskegee Airmen, for I didn't know too much about them. I never knew who her husband was until I was told about his remarkable life journey, although his life was cut short. Overall, I chose her not only because she is the grandmother of our good friends/cousins but also because she has an extensive memory of what happened almost 60 years ago.

Questions:
Q: How did you two meet? And where did you two go to school before/during the War?
A: Dudley Malone Watson, my husband, and I met in Columbia University in New York City. New York was my home before I moved to California, and Kentucky was Dudley's home. When he finished his schoolwork in the twelfth grade, he couldn't go to college in Kentucky because Kentucky didn't allow black students to go to college, so he was sent to Columbia University. At Kentucky, he was forced to write with his right hand, even though he was a lefty, due to prejudice. Before he graduated from Columbia at age 21, he got greetings letters from the army, but he was nervous because he didn't want to join the army because he loved the air force. He was so happy to find out that the air force wanted him, so that is how he became a Tuskegee Airmen.

Q: Where did he go during his training and combat?
A: He went directly to Tuskegee air force. In June 1942, he went into Tuskegee, and he was promoted to the May graduation because he was a great pilot. He graduated as a cadet instead of graduating as a private too. He became a Second Lieutenant in eighth months in training. I knew he went to Lockbourne, Ohio, Air Force Base to train first. This airbase was segregated, so there was a lot of tension. Next, he went to New Jersey, and here he got his promotion to First Lieutenant. The next assignment was in Presque Isle, Maine, for one year. We lived Nashville, Tennessee, for four years. In Tennessee, he was promoted to Major. I got many recommendations from the R.O.T.C. for him to go overseas. In June 1943, he was sent to Germany for both combat and delivery.

Q: What were his main duties as a Tuskegee Airmen? Do you remember his favorite memories?
A: His main jobs were head of R.O.T.C. and flying other places for combat or shipping cargo. He was called overseas to fly 101 missions to all of the places that the group was assigned. In these missions, his main duty was to protect the land that he was flying over. He was not wounded in battle. Yes, his most memorable memory was in Garmisch, Germany, where we stayed on vacation. While staying here my daughter learned to swim, and we could see the Alps. He would get up 5 a.m. to play golf with his friend, Max Robinson, rain or shine each morning at the air force base in Tennessee, where my uncle was born.

Student: Gregory Massimino-Garcia

Interviewed:Orsolina Massimino-Garcia for deceased grandfather Roman Massimino.

Relationship to student: Mother for grandfather

Date and location of interview: April 15, 2012 Pasadena, CA

I decided to interview my mother on behalf of my deceased grandfather since I had heard so little about him or who he was. I had known only a short story of him when he fought during the war, but that was it. I asked my mom about him and also found a giant photo book with a bunch of certificates and memorabilia. It was great to learn about who he was, what he did, and the part of my family I never knew about revealed to me.

What was he doing before he joined the military? He was an architect and interior decorator that lived in California and Monte Carlo, who got married during the war to a German-Austrian woman who saved his life as a prisoner of war, only to get re-married later on.

Was he enlisted or drafted? He was drafted on February 11, 1946 then released on August 6, 1947.

What did he do during the war? He was Airborne, so he jumped from planes, was an engineer building and repairing machines, was a photographer, and was part of a theatre group that provided entertainment during the lousy relaxing hours of the day.

Was he awarded any medals or citations? He was awarded the EAME Ribbon, Occupation Ribbon, and Victory Ribbon.

What was his everyday life like? He wrote letters telling his family about his experiences. There was not a lot of food, normally always the same thing to eat:

Hayden Boehle
Jess Santana
Great Uncle
04-21-12/Phone Interview (with help from daughter due to his dementia)

I chose to interview my uncle, Jess Santana, because he served in World War II. He was a pilot during the war and loved what he did. I was shocked to find out some of the things he did. I am proud to say he is my great uncle.

1. What were you doing before you joined the military?

I was living in West Los Angeles with my mother, sister and brother. I was going to UCLA. I was a quarterback on the football team. Jackie Robinson used to give me rides to school. I married my sweetheart Evagelina Pinedo before leaving for the war.

3. Did you enlist or were you drafted?

I wanted to work at Hughes Aircraft and I was turned down because I was Mexican American. I got so mad I promised myself I would show them by learning to fly one of their airplanes. I ended up joining the Army Air Corp and became a pilot! None of my friends enlisted with me. I had to take the street car to downtown Los Angeles to enlist since I didn't have a car. I thought it would be interesting and exciting to join the military. I was excited to get into an airplane. I even became a flight instructor.

4. What do you remember about your first days in the military?

I don't remember being lonely or scared because I was so excited about getting to fly airplanes. I was excited about being assigned to fly at some base in Europe and seeing parts of the world I had only dreamed about. I remember one day running low on fuel and had to return to base. The control tower told me I couldn't land and told me to go around. I finally got permission to land and I barely made it in. The airplane engine died just as I landed. My instructor never said anything to me! When I as stationed in Germany, I was able to fly with the Thunderbirds, a highly trained group of pilots who performed at air shows.

5. Where did you go during the war?

I first went to basic training in Texas and then flight school to learn how to fly airplanes. After that I was sent to North Africa during WWII. II flew C47 and C46 Cargo planes. I also flew B-25 aircraft. I transported airmen and soldiers, along with cargo and supplies. I lived in Casa Blanca and then I was transferred to Tripoli but I spent most of my time with military personnel. The days were long and there was no time for fun. It was a beautiful place but we were not there for a vacation, this was war. After the war I re-enlisted and I was stationed in Hawaii, Germany, Spain, and in the US. In Germany I flew the "Kinder Lift", which was a program that allowed German children to leave the battle torn city to vacation in Frankfurt.

9. What was your everyday life like?

I received letters from home and I wrote letters back. We weren't allowed to tell what we were doing but we could write about how much we missed our family. The food was always good because we were not on the battlefield. There was always plenty of supplies and equipment because the ships would bring them in along the coast and then we would load them in planes to take to the men on the battlefield. We lived in permanent buildings, not temporary tents like maybe the Army. Our beds were standard beds because we were pilots and officers assigned to a base. We didn't have time to feel homesick because we were so busy and we had a job to get done. Yes, I had pictures of my family above my bed. No, I was never superstitious nor did I have and "good luck charms" I always just said, "God willing, I would go here or there." I believed God's will would be done in my life. He watched over me and my family and thank God I returned from WWII.

Josh Liberto
Rowland Jalbert
Great Uncle
Sunday 22/4/12 Over the Phone

People who lived through the second Great War were those to be remembered. They are the people with the most amazing stories and the people we should aspire to be like. These people are many of our family members, yet as family we don't always take the time to ask about their war time experiences. My great uncle is a part of the greatest generation. He is a man with great intelligence and humility with his own experience which I had never heard before.

Prior to the bombing of Pearl Harbor he was a normal kid who like many others was not closely following the war in Europe, but still knew about the war in Europe. When the bombing happened he was home from high school recovering from a fractured ankle. This attack raised the questions of what would happen to everyone as well as to himself. He later joined the ROTC program at NYP and near after a semester he joined the reserves at Fort Devens in Massachusetts in March of 1943. There he was asked to join the Signal Core in the Air Core because of his desire to major in electrical engineering. He was sent to Robbins Field in Atlantic City for basic training where they were barracked in hotels that had been stripped of furniture so that it seemed more like a barrack. With the signal core he was a radio repair man. He was part of a team of fifteen people who would receive radio messages and be able to repair and set up radio towers. The interesting thing with these towers was that they were to be disguised silos so the enemy wouldn't bomb them. My great uncle thought it was weird that silos would be built in northern Africa because random silos in the desert would definitely look suspicious. During the war he was supposed to be sent to North Africa, Normandy, and Japan to set up radio towers, but the campaign ended sooner than they could leave. Ps. Hey uncle Roland this is a rough draft of what I'm writing. if you want you can cross out things you don't want in there or add anything. If you could also send a picture of yourself as you were in WWII that would be really great. Thanks for letting me interview. You can also call if you have any questions.

Questions
1. What were you doing before you joined the military?

College- nyp

Joined reserves

Joined fort Devens

- Where were you living?

Woonsocket Rhode Island

- Were you attending school?In Worcester
- Did you have a sweetheart?

Only after one semester in college with the rotc program

2. Do you remember how you felt about Japan or the war in Europe prior to Pearl Harbor?

Didn't have any troubled feelings. Didn't really follow events before pearl harbor. But was aware of what was going on. Being a kid didn't really watch it as closely as older people or as people who came from Europe. Started when he was in hs. Thought he was probably going to be involved. Considered it an adventure going to europe

- Do you remember the day pearl harbor was attacked?

He was home. Had been playing touch football in hs. Had a fractured ankle so he was nursing it. Cant say exactly what his reaction was. Probably excited. Already on the brink of war-excited about wondering what would happen to everybody. What would happen to him.

- Were you able to meet famous war heroes of the time? No not that he remembersDid you enlist or were you drafted?

What motivated you to enlist

Enlisted in the reserves. Was in the rotc

- Did any friends enlist with you

Friends from Wooster high school Where did you go to join?

Fort devens- mass---march of 43

Indoctrination point

Then the draft

Reserves weren't called up right away. Getting the draftees into the services

Asked those with electronic experience but didn't have much. But they saw that he wanted to study electrical engeneering. Sent to the signal core. He was a radio repair man. Team of 15 that handles messages, then installers, then the repair men

- Why did you choose you branch of service
- The army air core chose him
- What did you envision it would be like after you joined?
- What do you remember about your first days in the military?

Then a base in atlantic city. Barracked in the hotels. Fort lumm in new jersey the signal core

8   months. Then to Jefferson barrics. Was supposed to go to north Africa. Then to Normandy. Then to japan. some of the guys on the team went to seattle but he was still in Georgia. Do you remember anything from boot camp? How did it feel?

Student: Jesus Fugon

Veteran/Civilian interviewed: Mr. Kevin Dempsey on behalf of John Martin Dempsey (father), John Barton (grandfather), Elizabeth Dempsey (mother), and William Dempsey (Uncle).

Relationship to the student: Principal of middle school

Date and location of interview: 04/24/12 St. Agnes Parish School Main Office

Mr. Dempsey's grandfather, John Barton was Dutch and didn't enlist or was drafted to an army, but simply fought against the German occupant party in Holland. John Barton was a resistance fighter fighting against the oppressive Germans. During the war John Barton was in constant movement from fear of being caught by the Germans. He fought using Guerrilla tactics and traveling through the coast of Holland. He basically fought off handful of Germans and sometimes catching them alone. He once fought off a German taking his bayonet as a souvenir after he had killed him. When he saw that it was too dangerous he found a way to France taking a ship to New York. He then moved from New York to California finding a way back into the war. He was so passionate about the war that he tried to enlist for the Navy, but wasn't allowed due to the fact that he was an illegal immigrant at the time. He instead found a way into the Merchant Mariners without any knowledge whatsoever about being a sailor. He embarked as a barber, his true profession, but was mistaken for a cook. During one of his shipments that carried cargo to the U.S army, his ship was protected by naval ships and was soon attacked by the Japanese air force and submarines. The Kamikaze planes bombed one side of the ship and the submarine on the other side creating an explosion that destroyed the plane. Luckily, John Barton and a few other crew members drifted away to be picked up by one of the naval ships that protected the cargo shipment. After the war was over John Barton continued to live as a barber for the rest of his life.

Mr. Dempsey's father, John Martin Dempsey, had enlisted as Navy officer although he never saw combat due to his cataracts. He was stationed in San Pedro, California and eased town uprisings.

Mr. Dempsey's mother, Elizabeth Dempsey, was an ARP (Air Raid Precautions) Warden. Her job as an ARP Warden was to supervise the blackouts. The blackouts were total shut down of the cities lights due to better protection from aerial bombings from Japanese planes at the time. They had these precautions because of the fear that Japan might bomb any other city just how they had bombed Pearl Harbor. Her job was simple; she was to patrol the streets and to ensure that there was no visible light whatsoever. If the she saw any light she was responsible for alerting the people or person to turn the light off or to cover the window.

Mr. Dempsey's uncle, William Dempsey, was one of the B-52 pilots that bombed Dresden, Germany.

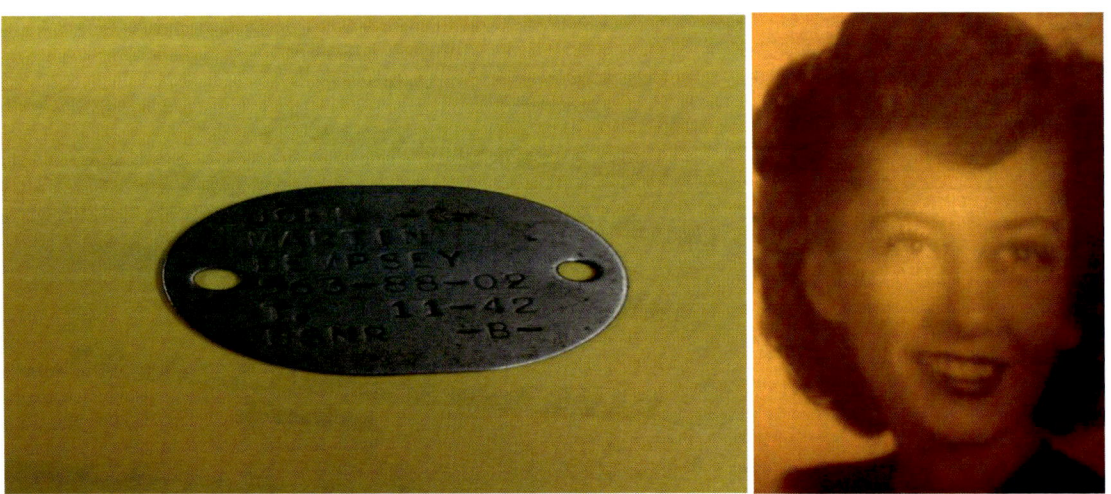

4.What was your first husband a part of?
~He was also in the air force and flew bombers.

5.What did you do during the war? Job?
~I was worked for a steel mill. I was in the office dealing with sales. I was valuable because I knew how to type. Boy did they put me to work…

6.We're you and/or other friends afraid of an invasion from the Germans or the Japanese?
~No, it wasn't even a thought.

7.What were people's attitudes about the war, we're some for it?
~We were all for it. Were called it Hitler's war and no one was against it. We felt that we needed to get rid of him.

8.What did you do when you heard that the war was over?
~Nothing, it was just another day for me.

9.What was it like to live during the 1940s?
~It was a lot of work. Food was hard to get, gas was hard to get, businesses were going out of business, and most of my friends businesses went bankrupt. People had to get special coupons in hour long lines to get the food that they needed.

10. What changed, for you, after the war was over?
~Nothing really changed except for my job. I didn't like office work. Being confined in a tiny workspace wasn't me. I became a dental assistant and that's were I met your grandpa.

Dylan Pinckert
Christine Pinckert
Grandma
4/13/12 The Fountains retirement home

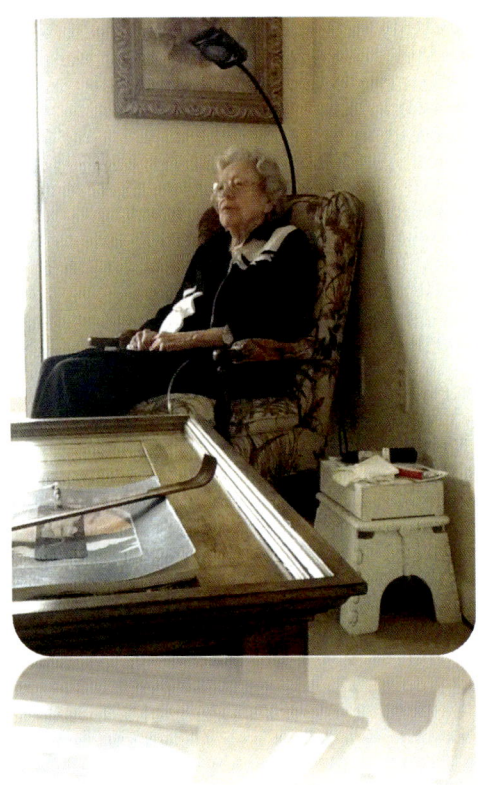 

1. We're people concerned about the soviet union during the war?
    ~Yes, we were all worried that they were going to join the Germans,
    same thing with China. We were all hoping they wouldn't join Japan.
    If they had joined Germany or Japan, we knew that we were
    screwed.

2. We're you directly affected by the war?
    ~My first husband was killed while bombing Berlin. He took a bullet
    from a German plane to the neck. He's buried in France.

3. What was opah a part of?
    ~He was in the air force. He was in the medical group and was a
    dentist. He would deal with the facial wounds.

Davis Waugh & Thomas Anastassiou

Davis Waugh – Loyola class of 2014

Portrait of Mr. Anastassiou done by a German POW

Davis Waugh
Mr. Line
World History 2
4/22/12

Student:	Davis Waugh
Veteran:	Thomas P. Anastassiou
Relationship to the student:	Family Friend

Date and location of interview: April 21, 2012, Rancho Palos Verdes, CA

I chose to interview Mr. Anastassiou because he is a friend of our family and is related to a person that works in my father's office. Also, Mr. Anastassiou did a lot of interesting things during WWII and I thought he would be the perfect person to speak with since he did everything from fight in combat to help with logistics and even help run a POW camp full of German prisoners.

1. What were you going before you joined the military?
He was attending Syracuse University with his brother James (who was killed in 1944 at Remagen Bridge during WWII) in Syracuse, New York. He was in Reserve Officer Training Corps (ROTC) at Syracuse.

2. What do you remember about your first days in the military?
On one of the first excursions he took with his platoon he fell under German artillery fire. He had his rifle blown in half and his canteen blown off. He was then chosen to teach the entire division of 16,000 men how to get in and out of a river crossing boat. Teaching is something Mr. Anastassiou really likes to do.

3. Where did you go during the war?
He spent the entire time in the Italian theatre from June, 1944 to the end of the war.

4. What where you doing during the war?
He saw combat in Italy and was wounded three times and won the Purple Heart. Then he applied and got a posting at the allied headquarters in Italy working on the allied use of petroleum for the war effort. He was awarded the rank of captain for discovering that England wasn't paying their share of the petroleum - this saved the U.S an estimated eight billion dollars.

5. Were you awarded any metals or citations?
He was awarded the Purple Heart, and the Foreign Occupation medal.

6. What was your everyday life like?
He wrote many letters home to his family and received many from his father, who was a Greek Orthodox Priest. The food for officers was very good. He said this was an improvement over home life since they were a very poor family. His first meal was fried chicken and a coke. The living conditions were hard when on the front line, but otherwise they were good. They lived in tents and occasionally got to stay in hotel rooms when they captured a city. He didn't carry any reminders of home with him nor did he have any lucky charms.

Student: Jeremy Bjelajac
Civilian Interviewed: Patricia Devine
Relationship to student: Grandparent
Date and Location of Interview: 4/22/12. Over the phone.

        I chose to interview my grandmother about her experience with World War II because I had always heard her mention one or to things, but I never asked her for the whole story. I also wanted to interview her because I can pass on this information on to my children and help keep the stories of the Greatest Generation alive. This assignment really helped me to get a better view of what life was like in the times of war. I have learned that people from my generation and those from the Greatest Generation have many different views on life because they grew up in much darker circumstances. The Greatest Generation certainly have some great stories to tell and I thoroughly enjoyed hearing them.

- **Where were you living when WW2 started?** New York City. I was in elementary school.
- **How old were you when the war started?** I was 12 years old.
- **What school were you attending?** I went to Good Shepard.
- **How did you feel when Pearl Harbor was attacked?**
  Awful. I remember my dad was silent that night. We
  heard it on radio. It was Sunday night, and we were
  eating dinner.
- **Did you have any close friends that were drafted or
  enlisted?** No I didn't because I was too young to know
  men who were that old. When things got more and more
  crazy, the U.S. started to draft men up to 40 years old. I
  had a cousin that went. He was in the battle of Bulls in
  Germany. After that he was sent to Africa. When he got
  back he was so different from what I remember.
- **What was everyday life like being a younger person in
  the States during this time?** Well my Father had the job
  of checking the curtains to make sure no light was going
  through to the outside. I never understood why he did
  this. As for supplies we were running low on everything
  from tin foil to meat and even shoes. Many businesses
  changed to fit the needs of Americans in that time. I
  remember the only way to get shoes was to give the lady
  at the register a coupon. The one positive was that
  everybody stuck together. They were United and it was a
  great thing to see in those horrible times.
- **Was there any nervousness or fear that another
  attack would hit the U.S ?** I myself did not not hear
  much about the war, but I had neighbors that were
  German who were arrested for transmitting messages
  back and forth to Germany. I also met a Japanese woman

that was kidnapped and sent to Manzanar for three years. Her father died there and when they got back to the U.S. her house was taken away and sold. The worst part was that her brother was fighting for the U.S. while all of this was going on.
- **Do you remember the day of V-E day or V-J day?** Oh yes. It was a great day. I was working downtown at the age of 16. People were running through streets and hugging each other. I had never seen so much joy. At the time I was working for a phone company and the manager was so happy he let everyone go home to their families and take the day off.
- **How different was normal life when the war ended?** It took a while to get back to normal. It was a time when everyone looked forward to getting new jobs. I read in the paper that people who were in the war wanted to go to California to work and start a new life.

Kurt Weber
Willy Weber speaking on behalf of Heinz Weber
Father (Willy Weber) speaking on behalf of Grandfather (Heinz Weber)
Sunday, April 22, 2012 in Los Angeles, California

   I chose to interview my father (speaking about my grandfather) because I never got to meet my grandfather because he died of cancer before I was born, and I thought that it would be interesting to learn more about my grandfather. I always knew that my grandfather fought in World War II, but I never knew any of the details. The only thing I knew about my grandfather before this interview was that my grandfather fought for Germany, but he was against the Nazi's and Hitler's beliefs. I had no clue what my grandfather's life was like before, during, and after the war. I didn't even know how my grandfather met my grandmother.

Q. What was grandpa doing before he joined the military? Where did he live?

A. He was in an engineering school to be a machinist in 1942. He was born, raised, and lived in Leipzig, Germany.

Q. Did grandpa enlist or was he drafted? When was he enlisted or drafted? Where was he enlisted or drafted? How old was he when he was enlisted or drafted?

A. He was not in support with what Hitler was doing in the war, but he was drafted on April 14, 1942. He reported to his local drafting station in the city of Leipzig. He was 18 years old.

Q. What branch of service did grandpa serve in?

A. He ended up in the 87th Infantry Division of the German army (Wehrmacht).

Q. How did he feel about the war? Was it hard for him? Was there enough food? Was he ever stressed?

A. He didn't like the war, and he didn't like talking about the war either, but he was forced to be in the war because of the law. It was a very difficult time. Grandpa told my dad that soldiers would reach into their armpits and pull out a handful of lice. There was enough food to survive on, but the food wasn't plentiful. He declined becoming an officer because they rarely survived capture by the Russians. His Iron Cross also made him a target for vengeful Russians.

Q. Where did grandpa go during the war? How did he get there?

A. He was sent to the Russian Front by train. He was sent to Rzhez.

Q. Did grandpa ever get hurt during the war?

A. He got wounded in his upper arm on August 28, 1942. It took him one year to recover from his injury.

Q. What did grandpa do during the war?

A. He fought at Rzhev, Russia. The Russians took over Rzhev which is just about 100 miles west of Moscow.

Q. Was grandpa ever captured?

A. He was captured by the Russians in the Kurland pocket in May 1945. That pocket was among the last Germans to surrender. He was captured because Hitler didn't believe in retreating. He spent 3 years as a Russian prisoner of war.

Q. Was grandpa awarded any medals or citations?

A. He was awarded the Iron Cross 2nd Class on March 27, 1944. Then he was awarded the Silver Infantry Assault Medal on March 20, 1944. He was awarded the Black Wounded Award on September 11, 1942.

Q. Did grandpa write many letters home? What did he do to pass the time?

A. Yes, he wrote many letters to his parents back in Leipzig. To pass the time, he played skat, the German card game.

Q. Was grandpa allowed to go back home to Leipzig?

A. Yes. He was sent home after he got wounded.

Q. What did the end of the war mean to grandpa?

A. The end of the war was his way of being released from the Russians. It also meant life because he was very sick.

Q. What was his life like after the war?

A. He spent one year in a hospital recovering. There were no jobs in Germany due to the devastation of the war. His aunt was living in Thailand which was relatively untouched by the war, and he moved there in 1949. There he met my grandma around 1951.

Student: Reuben Peters
Civilian Interviewed: Beverly (97 years old) and her daughter Judy
Relationship to the Student: Neighbor
Date and location of the interview: Neighbors house; 4/21/12 12:30 AM
I chose my civilian because she was a good age to remember the war she also had a daughter that lived during the time also. She also had close ones that served during the war also.

Q. What area were you living during World War 2?

A. We lived in Waterloo, Idaho and when I was four (Judy) we moved to West Los Angles.

Q. Where you attending school?

A. No I was not I was twenty-two at the time and worked in the Santa Monica hospital as a nurse. My daughter was four at the time.

Q. Did you have a sweetheart?

A. Yes I did, I met my fist husband Harris Thomason who I was married to for twenty-two years. One day my husband said to me he was not feeling to well and I said, " I can see" so I took him to the hospital and he ended up dieing of a heart attack. However I met my other husband Bill and we got married at age forty-four.

Q. Did any of your siblings fight in World War 2?

A. Yes my husband Bill served four years for the Air force and he was stationed here in California and did not go over seas however my brother had to fight in Germany. In Germany he was ridding in a tank it blew up and all of his hair and body was burnt and he had to hold still and watch as the Germany solders checked if he was dead. My brother received an award and got a chance to meet the queen of England for his bravery. My uncle also served during World War 2 for the navy.

Q. What was life like during World War 2?

A. We had a certain curfew and the lights in the whole city would go off to prevent any enemy planes from bombing the city. We also had to have these blinds on our windows to prevent light from entering and no one was allowed to have any lights on. There were also army men in these dugouts around the Santa Monica pier protecting us in case of any invasions.

Q. How was food like during World War 2?

A. Food was not too much of an issue but it all had to rationed out to all of the people because the men overseas needed food also.

Q. Did most men during World War 2 enlist into the war or were they drafted?

A. I'm not sure but my husband Bill was drafted and because of that he was not able to go to collage. So he had to leave his family that was having a tough time financially. I do remember buses full of men headed to the war.

Q. Did you write or receive any letters from your husband or uncle?

A. Yes I did my first husband Harris Thomas would write me letters that were censured I would write back also.

Q. Did any one you know go through any life or death experiences during the war?

A. Yes, my second husband Bill was flying in a plane with his unit and the plane was shot down and it crashed but luckily all of them survived. They had to watch there plane burst up in flames.

Student: Cesar E. Castro

Civilian Interviewed: Maria S.

Relationship to the student: Friend

Date and location of the interview: April 21, 2012. The interview was in Los Angeles over the phone to New York City.

When I first began my project, I chose to interview my neighbor, Santiago. However, I learned that he did not have a great deal of information; therefore he referred me to his friend. Santiago's friend, Maria S., was delighted of the project I was doing. When Ms. S. informed me that her husband was an interpreter for the Allies, I was astonished and excited to interview her. I began thinking of all the historical people that Mr. S. might have interpreted for. Since Ms. S. lives in New York City, I performed my interview over the phone with her.

Q. When and where were you born?

A. I was born in Germany in 1929.

Q. Who was your husband?

A. My husband was Tony S. and he was an interpreter for the Allies during World War 2.

Q. Did he enlist or was he drafted into the military?

A. He enlisted to join the military and the military leaders chose him because he knew many languages. He spoke Spanish, English, French, German, Italian, Russian, Chinese, Japanese, Hungarian, and Polish.

Q. Where did he go during the war?

A. Well he was stationed in Germany from 1945-1947 and he was with the occupational troops. He traveled with troops because he spoke many languages and was able to speak with people from different countries.

Q. What was your everyday life like during the war?

A. My everyday life was terrible once the bombing started. Many times we went to a cellar to be safe. There were some terrible bombings and many people were killed. I remember one night it was very cold and the few fire engines could not put out all the fire. I also remember there were air mines and fire bombs. Where I lived, the windows were broken so we could not stay there. So we just started walking with people to some houses that were still standing. That was the worst experience.

http://www.youtube.com/watch?v=u3uAU97q_6k&context=C477f6aeADvjVQa1PpcFPIV9hR_qnzCQ3tZoRhuqD51ItJc1StmMY=

http://www.youtube.com/watch?v=BctlFVcMFtU&context=C4c361dcADvjVQa1PpcFPIV9hR_qnzCdn3Y2YmZOwQtMRYtqtDf3c=

Tino Altieri
Mr. Line
World History Period 4
23 April 2012

Q&A Interview

My name is Tino Altieri and the World War two veteran whom I interviewed is my grandpa Russel Summler. I interviewed him via email and I am very thankful for my gradfather's presence in this world. Grandpa Russel fought in the war for three years as a member of the army and with the education of how to fly a jet. The date of this interview was April 19, 2012. My grandpa was mainluy stationed around the United States, but also fought in the Philippines.

1. Do you remember how you felt about Japan or the war in Europe prior to Pearl Harbor?
-Dou you remember how you felt the day Pearl Harbor was attacked?
-Were you able to me famous war heroes of the time?
1 .Prior to Pearl Harbor I was in high school and I spent a lot of time following Hitler in Germany, my grandfather came from there and his heart was still there. We had only radio and news reels that you saw where ever you could. I remember feeling nothing positive about his leadership but he had many followers in all areas of the world that bought into his antics. I was very disturbed the day of Pearl Harbor at Japan, for the attack, but also I remember I felt many in US leadership dropped the ball, the world was at war, we were building up the military with men and equipment and our perimeter was not alert and secure. I had a brother and many friends in the military service so I had skin in the game. In my 87 years on this planet I have crossed path with many that have made the headlines and I have found that most are there through their own PR people. The people I try break bread with are those made this world much better than they found it. Tino, remember the young man and the starfish fable.

2. What do you remember about your first days in the military?
-Do you remember anything from boot camp?
-Were you nervous, scared, excited?
-Do you remember anything about your instructors?
-Did you do any advanced training?
-What do you remember about the other people in your unit?
 2. I entered the military eager but very apprehensive. The great adjustment was bunking down with a cross section of people on the street, one has to be prepared for anything. The instructors at that time tried to instill discipline by breaking the recruits to zero, I did not felt it worked then. Leadership is leading not driving. I took advantage of all advanced training available from mechanical, technical, leadership…with emphasis on skills I could use after the war such as flying an airplane. You meet a lot good people but I found out early not to get too close for most of the time you move alone.

3. Where did you go during the war? -Where were you stationed first? (Do you remember the trip there?
-Do you remember when you first arrived at the new location?
Did you travel to other places?
3. My entrance to the Army was from the farm in Illinois to my first station in Georgia, which we traveled to by train, through places I had never been and I was excited and probably scared. On arrival at Camp Stewart we were greeted and the training started, I was in a strange world for me.

4. What were you doing during the war?
-What jobs or assignments did you have?
-Did you see combat?
-Can you tell me about your most memorable experiences?
-Were you awarded any medals or citation and how did you earn them?
4. I moved many times during the three years in the Army. From the Aircraft Artillery in Ga to Air Force pilot training in Mississippi and Oklahoma A&M, then Cheyenne Wyo ,then Virginia, then California, then throughout Philippine Islands and last stop Japan. My assignments were many and varied, no heroic medals were bestowed or earned, we all received recognition for being in the combat zones at various times, I would not consider myself a combat veteran. Right or wrong. I am still not positioned on the dropping of the A-Bomb{I *visited the area}* , we were stationed in Northern Philippines waiting for the invasion of Japan. My memorable experience is the insight on people, the egg & sperm are important the day you are born and from that day forward look in the mirror and that person sets the course of your life. My experience has proved to me that the people that have instilled The Cowboy Code of Ethics and that have a purpose and goal do not have time for social pettiness.

5. What was it like after the war?
-What are your first memories of going home>
-Did you go to school and did you take advantage of the GI bill?
-Where were you living?
-What work did you do, how did your career develop after that?
5. On homecoming your family and friends welcomed you with open arms but the rest of society sort of said get a life the war is over. On reflection, that is probably way it should be. I felt it was a world bigger than Russell Charles and if I was going to leave my mark I should get with it and before my discharge I enrolled in a college that was open at that time. I took advantage of the GI bill but I found out early that with time management I could carry a full schedule and work full time and become asset solvent on graduation. I realized quickly that my degree in physics and political science was on the beginning and I spent the next 14 years in night school covering law, finance, accounting, management ....while I had a work career of teaching, clerking. selling, construction and building businesses.
TINO—Life is good, but not always fair, just remember always enjoy the journey and make the man in the mirror proud of you.
Grandpa Russ

Alex Alvarado
Angel S. Alvarado
Grandparent
13 April, 2012 Pico Rivera, CA

Due to my grandfather's worsening condition of Alzheimer's, I knew his memory of the war would soon be lost forever. As a result, I wanted to preserve his perspective throughout this amazing point in his life. Although he wasn't able to remember what he ate for breakfast, he could tell me exactly the school he went to, what day he stormed the beach, and where he went after he landed. Some of the answers I was given from my grandpa surprised me and gave me a new light to view my grandfather in. Also, despite knowing some facts about his service already, I got a more complete picture of the time he spent in the Army.

Q: What were you doing before you joined the military?
A: I was going to school, St. Mary's Moraga
Q: Where were you living?
A: On campus at St. Mary's
Q: Did you have a sweetheart?
A: No

Q: Do you remember anything from bootcamp?
A: (Laughing) I washed a lot of dishes
Q: How was it physically? Was it demanding? What were some of the training exercise you did?
A: Oh yah very much. We used to run, march, and exercise a lot. We were in good shape.
Q: How did it feel when you were in boot camp, were you nervous, scared, excited?
A: I just took it in stride.
Q: Do you remember anything about your instructors?
A: I remember Lt. Wyatt was a nice guy; Lt. Hoff was not too hot.
Q: Can you describe them?
A: Lt. Wyatt was a nice guy, tall; He had been at Texas A & M. And Lt. Hoff was from Georgie I think, and he thought he was God's gift to humanity

Q: Where did you go during the war? You landed at Normandy correct?
A: Yes?
Q: Were in the first waves to hit the beaches?
A: No
Q: But there was still pretty heavy fire going on?
A: Oh yah. I came on D-Day plus 6.
Q: Do you remember the trip there? What was that like especially when the gate dropped from the boat and you jumped into the ocean?
A: Well, you just go.
Q: It was just training kicked in?
A: I guess so
Q: Did you travel to any other places?
A: Yah we went to some small French towns and eventually worked our way into Paris; After that, we went through Belgium and towards Germany. I was stationed in Frankfurt after the war.

Q: Were you awarded any medals or citations?
A: Yes sir, I was awarded a purple heart and an iron cross.
Q: What was the iron cross for?
A: Supposedly for bravery
Q: Do you remember for what occasion you earned that for?
A: Well we just moved forward that's all.
Q: What do these medals mean to you?
A: Well they're there.
Q: You don't see them as anything important?
A: Well, just that, well, I got them that's all. Something had to be done that's all.
Q: What do you hope to do with these medals?
A: Give them to you one day

Q: What was your everyday life like?
A: First of all we stayed in our foxholes. We would get out, walk around a bit, then hop back in when we got the chance
Q: Did you write many letters home?
A: Not to many.
Q: The couple that you did write, do you remember who to or what you said?
A: Nani Fina (my great-aunt)
Q: What was the food like?
A: Lousy but we ate it
Q: Did you always get enough food?
A: Oh yah
Q: What were some of your other supplies and equipment:
A: My M1 Garand, my boots, my winter clothes, my bazooka.
Q: What were your living conditions like?
A: Well we would be in our foxholes for up to a month so we rarely got to shower.
Q: Were there times when you felt homesick or stressed?
A: No, my mother and father had both already passed on and all I had was my older sister, so I didn't really get homesick
Q: Did you carry any reminders of home with you?
A: I might have had a couple of pictures here and there
Q: Did you believe in any "good luck charms" or superstitions?
A: (Shaking his head) No.

Wil Bakula
Barbara Botfield
Grandmother
April 4th 2012 at Barbara's House

I chose to interview my Nan (Nan is the word for Grandmother in England) Barbara Botfield, who lived during the time of WWII in England. She lived through all of the war, beginning to end, and has the most interesting stories out of all my family members who have lived during that time. She is also the only one that has the European perspective on the war. She stayed in America after moving here after the war, and now lives in Burbank, CA. The following are a few of the questions and answers from the 35-minute interview I conducted at her house.

W: What were you doing before the war started?

B: Before the war started, I had just turned 14, and the war had started in 1939. I had just left All Saints High School, I had started working at a jewelry store. The night the war started I was at a carnival, and they had just roasted a big pig and I had had one of their sandwiches. Then the paper boy was running around saying, "Extra, Extra. War has been declared." And it kind of scared me a little bit, but mostly before that I was in school. We had long days at school. After the war started, nothing much happened for the first year. But then one night the sirens went off, so we ran down to the cellar which my dad had built with extra structures to act as a bomb shelter, and my mom had put cots down there. But nothing really happened except we could hear the planes going over.

W: Where were you living at the time?

B: I was living in West Bromwich, which is like the Midlands, and the Midlands is the Birmingham area of England. And its also where the made the MG cars, but when the war started, they stopped making cars and made airplanes. So naturally I thought the Germans were trying to find that place.

W: What did you feel about the war in Europe prior to Pearl Harbor?

B: Well, I really didn't know much about Pearl Harbor because Hitler had walked into Poland and all the countries in Europe and France had just given up. He was only a few miles across the English Channel. I used to have dreams that the airplanes would come over and chase me up the street, and I would wake up sweating. So then I joined the ambulance service, and one of the reasons I joined that was that everyone was in uniform and even though I was supposed to be 17, I told them my wrong age. So if the sirens went off, the dispatched a driver and an assistant to the first aid services so when the sirens went off and people got hurt, they would go to these first aid services instead of the hospital. In the ambulance service is also where I met your grandfather, who was a driver. I asked the director if he would put me with this new driver, but he said "No I will not." But I still met him and that's how I met your grandfather.

W: Even after the war, Britain was still in bad shape?

B: Yes, things were still rationed. We had 2 ounces of butter a week. 2 ounces! That's like how much I put on a pat of toast now! They started building up Europe before they started building up new roads and things in England.

W: During the war did you see any kind of combat?

B: Yes, one night I had left where I was working and I had gone to go see a movie called Irene (you can find it on Imdb). So I was in there for a little while but then it came on the screen: "the sirens have sounded, but stay in here you are safer here then in the streets." But then after a while, I was in the balcony, and the people down below jumped up and started screaming saying that a bomb and dropped through the roof like a buzz bomb. I jumped up to go out because I was scared, so I ran down stairs and the air raid warden at the bottom of the stairs told me that the buses to where I was living had stopped hours ago and that I should run to an air raid shelter. He said that one was right around the corner so I ran right around the corner and ran down the stairs to the shelter. Just as I ran down the stairs, a big bomb went off really close and the air came down the stairs and blew my dress right over my head. So I ran in there, and people kept coming in and saying to others, "Oh Susie, your house is gone, Rachel, your house is gone," because it had landed so close. I walked around with some boys because the whole town was still on fire, and then I ran all the way home which was about 4 miles away. Little did I know that my father and brother were on their bikes, biking around looking for me because they thought that I could be dead.

Youtube link: Part 1 - http://youtu.be/QNU1QPaJlrE (links for part 2-5 are located on the videos)

Student: Chris Brown

Veteran Interviewed: Thomas Robert Brown (through my dad)

Relationship to me: Grandfather

Date and location of interview: 4/22/12

I chose to interview my grandfather because he grew up right when World War II was starting. As a teenager in high school, he along with many others felt it was their duty to serve their country by joining the war effort. He is a patriotic man and is very proud to be honored as a veteran of World War II.

Do you remember how you felt about Japan or the war in Europe prior to Pearl Harbor?

Prior to Pearl Harbor he didn't know much about Japan or their culture and thus was indifferent about the Japanese. In regards to the war in Europe, he was very supportive towards the cause, and strongly felt that the U.S. should help to eliminate Hitler's regime. My grandfather doesn't remember much, but he does remember the day Pearl Harbor was bombed, and "anger" was the only word to describe what my grandfather felt about it. Despite the bombings, some of my grandfather's best friends after the war were Japanese.

Did you enlist or were you drafted? What motivated you to join?

My grandfather enlisted in Pittsburg as a senior in high school. His motivation came from his support in the cause of the war and the love and loyalty for his country. He, his brothers and his friends from school enlisted, though they were not put in the same unit. My great uncle George was one of my grandfather's brothers that enlisted with him.

Where did you go during the war?

During the war, my grandfather went to Germany where he was stationed for a few years. He, along with thousands more, was shipped into Europe across the Atlantic ocean via the *Queen Mary*. According to him, the trip there took about 12 days, and it was so crowded that soldiers were sleeping outside on the deck of the boat because it was so crowded. He stayed at Germany, although his brother, George, was shipped to fight the Pacific campaign.

What was your everyday life like?

Because my grandfather was never engaged in combat, everyday life in Europe wasn't that bad. He lived in the military barracks, and they always had a sufficient amount of decent quality food. He would write home often, keeping in touch with his mom, his dad, and his sister. In the letters, he told that he was very homesick and missed everyone very much. To remind himself of home, he carried small pictures of his family and close friends.

What was it like after the war?

After the war, he was shipped back to Pittsburg, but realized there were more job opportunities in the west coast and moved to California. He took a train across America to Los Angeles where he and his brothers and sister founded a carpet company named "Brown Brother's Carpet co." his sister, Betty, would run the office and he and his brothers would do the manual labor.

Student: Chancellor Ramirez

Civilian Interviewed: Peter Scamagas

Relation to the Student: Best Friends Grandpa

Date and Location of the Interview: April 20, 2012

I chose to interview my civilian because I thought it would be interesting to learn more about a person who lived in Europe and not the US. Once when I found out that Jack's grandpa lived during World War II in Greece, I was immediately interested and wanted to learn more. I'm happy I interviewed Mr. Peter Scamagas.

1. What was your everyday life like once when the war started?

I continued to go to school and continue my everyday life. All of the children of the town knew to always stay out of the Germans way. Also, Instead of being able to eat I had to go sneak and crawl through the minefields and get food.

2. Did you stay in Greece for the entire war?

Yes, I was born in Philadelphia and moved to the Island of Chios, Greece. I was with my sister for a large part of the war.

3. Did your life change once when the war was over?

Yes, after the war I moved back to America with my sister, but I was left with only a few pennies. The war took a hard toll on my family and left us with very little.

4. How did the Germans treat you and your town?

For every 1 German officer that was killed, 10 island women of the village were killed. The people of the village knew to stay out of the Germans way in order to stay out of harms way.

5. Were you and your family able to live in the same home the entire war?

The Germans took over our house, which was located in the middle of the town. Our house was in the better part of the town. Once when the Germans took over, we were forced to move to the outskirts of the town. We were forced to move in with our servant's family.

Q: Do you remember V-E Day and V-J Day when the war ended?

A: "I just remember hearing on the radio that we had won the war in Europe and Japan and people were screaming THE WAR IS OVER!"

Q: How did you celebrate the end of the war?

A: "We didn't really celebrate the end of the war because my parents weren't the celebrating type."

Steven Chaves

Jacqueline Patricia Nicholson- Sacco

Grandmother

April 20, 2012

I thought my grandmother, an Italian American, was a perfect fit for this project because she lived during World War II. I don't know anyone who actually fought in the war and she is the only living person close enough to me to share her personal thoughts, feelings, and experience during this great time. She lost close friends, her life style changed drastically, and memory of this historical time.

Q: During the war did you have to move?

A: "Yes. Until 1942 I lived in a two story six bedroom, two bathroom house in New Jersey. When we moved out here I lived in a one bedroom apartment and shared a bathroom with six other people."

Q: Did you have any prize possessions during this time?

A: "When I was 5 my grandmother gave me a 1942 doll that I took everywhere."

Q: Did you lose any of your friends during the war?

A: "My cousin fought in the war. He was a fighter pilot that was shot down near the English war was over and was never the same. He became an alcoholic and eventually committed suicide."

Student: Jack Grover
Civilian Interviewed: Katina Scamagas
Relationship to the student: Yiayia(Grandma)
Date of Interview: Friday April 20, 2012
Opening: I had always known that my Yiayia had an interesting history and she had always told me bits and pieces of her story. I wanted to get the full story of what this experience was like. She said she was opened to any question I wanted to ask, so I asked away.

What was your first experience like with the Germans?
I was a young girl, about 6 or 7 years old, and my father brought me to the German officers and he asked me to speak German, and they clapped. Then he asked me to count and they gave me candy. The other kids in my village were jealous.

Did you have to deal with any other countries during German occupation or was it Germany alone?
Well before the Germans came we were fighting the Italians. We were able to hold them off. Then the Germans came. They had much better technology and weapons.

And how were the Italians compared to the Germans?
They were not as into the war as the Germans. They were not as advanced with there weapons, but they both treated me pretty well, especially because I had uncle who was a commander.

How did your everyday life change?
Well, I was a pretty young girl so not much changed for me, but because at the time Communism was starting to become prevalent. My dad was a speaker against them and was constantly being hunted down. This is when my life really started to change because we had to go from house to house throughout Sparta and hide. Unfortunately he was killed.

Was it the Communist that killed him?
Well, the Communist did not do it themselves. They told the town drunk that the girl he (the drunk) was in loved that he would not have a chance with her as long as my father was alive. Thank God that my uncle was able to take care of my brother and me.

Student: Brett Rasic

Veteran/Civilian interviewed: Robert Mounts

Relationship: Grandpa

Date and Location Interviewed: 4/21/12 Glendora, grandpa's house

-What where you doing before you joined the military?

- I was living in St. Luis with my two brothers and I had been out of high school for a few years, but there really wasn't any work so at the time and the military was paying ok if you joined, so we all joined the military and were sent off to Michigan for training.

- What where you doing in the war?

- When my brothers and I went to training camp together, they assigned me a browning light machine gun, because I was one of the stronger men at camp. So during combat I had two jobs. One was to man my machine gun and the other was to record bombing days and times in a journal.

- Where you awarded any medals or citations?

- During the war I received a bronze medal for save my best friend, who was wounded in the leg.   I carried him and all my gear to the medic where he was saved and sent home. It's not the medal that means something to me it's the fact that I saved my best friend from harm's way.

-What was your everyday life like?

- I didn't write to many letters, and when I did they were to my other brother seeing how they were and making sure they were ok. The food we got was always crap except sometime we would get chocolate bars which we would trade the locals for to do our laundry. Where I was fighting it was really moist so they always told us to have dry socks on us because sometimes it rained for days. I didn't really believe in good luck charms beside the crucifix.

- What did you do to pass the time?

- Most of my time off I had I wrote in my journal that I had to keep with me at all times because it had all the bombing times and dates in it. Some time if we were lucky would get a deck of card and play cards for cigarettes.

Lorenzo Secci
Civilian:
Relationship to Me: Great Aunt
Date and Location: 24 April 2012; Phone Call

I chose to interview my great aunt because she is one of the only family members that I have left that lived and survived throughout WWII. I am very close with her and I always see her at family events and holidays.

Q: What were you doing before the war?
A: I was going to elementary school in San Donato, a small village just eighteen miles outside of Florence. I was only seven years old when they told me our country was going to war.

Q: What do you remember about when the war first started.
A: I didn't really understand what was really happening because I was so little. What I remember more vividly was the Germans left and shortly after the Americans came. I was only ten years old and we had to move out of our house because the Americans were bombing us.

Q: Where did you go during the war?
A: I stayed in my village, it was too dangerous to travel anywhere else. There was no common way of traveling. All the roads were blocked off and there were no trains.

Q: What was your everyday life like?
A: Bad times. If you don't go through war you don't know what its like. I was afraid of everything, sometimes my mom would cry and I didn't really know why because I was so young. I became an older person through the war because I had to worry about many things. There was dynamite all around our house because the Germans wanted to blow up a bridge that led into Vienna. My dad and older brother would go around one o'clock in the morning and pour water on the dynamite so it wouldn't explode and destroy our house. The food was scarce but luckily my dad had a mill that made wheat. So we would sell the wheat to other neighbors and in return get other goods and foods.

Q: What was life like after the war?
A: It was a relief, but the country was still very poor. I felt like I was young again because I had nothing to worry about. Life was easier and I stopped being afraid of other militaries.

Q: Who were his main friends and comrades that he met in camps/training or in his fleet? Were there any casualties of his friends?

A: His close friends were Benjamin O. Davis, Max Robinson, and Jimmy Walker and the rest of the members in his unit that I can't remember exactly. Dudley Watson was an officer, but during his time in the air force, there was prejudice, so there was much tension between the white and the black members of the army. Jimmy Walker was one casualty in his unit, for he was shot down. The Tuskegee Airmen didn't have any casualties in the war, for the only time where these men died was after the war.

Q: Did he ever write letters to you? Did he have any complaints about the food or supplies? Also was he very homesick?

A: I wrote letters to him every single week. I talked about both of our families, what I was doing, what new people I'd met, and letters about everyday life. He wrote about day-to-day situations, not much about combat. He wrote about things in the air force bases in Germany, but he did not write much about the combat in the war. He never complained about how the food was like in the air force bases. I am not good cook, and my husband didn't complain about the taste of my food as long as he ate something. I remember he said that all supplies or equipment that he needed for his duties, the air force would give it to him. If he needed some repairs in the planes, the air force commanders would supply. There were times where he felt homesick. He always wrote letters to me every week to see how everyone at home was doing. He was not superstitious and didn't really carry any "good luck charms", but he was very serious in his duties. He just did what he needed to do, and he succeeded in his roles.

I will never forget, on January 20th, 1958, he had to fly 4 hours every night to stay on "flying pay." He flew at 6:00 p.m. to 10:00 p.m. for readiness (in case of attacks). This night, he died in a plane accident around 9:00 p.m. At 12:00 midnight, the Chaplin and my husband's friend Benjamin O. Davis and his wife came to tell me that my husband has passed away. Dudley was flying as a copilot and the main pilot, Mr. Richardson, had difficulties with the plane. They almost made the landing, but the plane unfortunately exploded.

Matthew Young
Mrs. Bernice Watson
My Cousin's Grandmother
April 22, 2012. San Pedro, California

I chose to interview Mrs. Bernice Watson because I knew she has a great memory on the memories with her and her deceased husband. I thought it would be a great opportunity for me to gain more knowledge of the Tuskegee Airmen, for I didn't know too much about them. I never knew who her husband was until I was told about his remarkable life journey, although his life was cut short. Overall, I chose her not only because she is the grandmother of our good friends/cousins but also because she has an extensive memory of what happened almost 60 years ago.

Questions:
Q: How did you two meet? And where did you two go to school before/during the War?
A: Dudley Malone Watson, my husband, and I met in Columbia University in New York City. New York was my home before I moved to California, and Kentucky was Dudley's home. When he finished his schoolwork in the twelfth grade, he couldn't go to college in Kentucky because Kentucky didn't allow black students to go to college, so he was sent to Columbia University. At Kentucky, he was forced to write with his right hand, even though he was a lefty, due to prejudice. Before he graduated from Columbia at age 21, he got greetings letters from the army, but he was nervous because he didn't want to join the army because he loved the air force. He was so happy to find out that the air force wanted him, so that is how he became a Tuskegee Airmen.

Q: Where did he go during his training and combat?
A: He went directly to Tuskegee air force. In June 1942, he went into Tuskegee, and he was promoted to the May graduation because he was a great pilot. He graduated as a cadet instead of graduating as a private too. He became a Second Lieutenant in eighth months in training. I knew he went to Lockbourne, Ohio, Air Force Base to train first. This airbase was segregated, so there was a lot of tension. Next, he went to New Jersey, and here he got his promotion to First Lieutenant. The next assignment was in Presque Isle, Maine, for one year. We lived Nashville, Tennessee, for four years. In Tennessee, he was promoted to Major. I got many recommendations from the R.O.T.C. for him to go overseas. In June 1943, he was sent to Germany for both combat and delivery.
Q: What were his main duties as a Tuskegee Airmen? Do you remember his favorite memories?
A: His main jobs were head of R.O.T.C. and flying other places for combat or shipping cargo. He was called overseas to fly 101 missions to all of the places that the group was assigned. In these missions, his main duty was to protect the land that he was flying over. He was not wounded in battle. Yes, his most memorable memory was in Garmisch, Germany, where we stayed on vacation. While staying here my daughter learned to swim, and we could see the Alps. He would get up 5 a.m. to play golf with his friend, Max Robinson, rain or shine each morning at the air force base in Tennessee, where my uncle was born.

David Mariscal
L.B. Strawn
WWII Veteran and Poet
4/23/12 at Strawn Residence in Cerritos

A Generation of Service

Meeting and interviewing Mr. L.B. Strawn was an experience that I will never forget. I met Mr. Strawn through a family friend. Mr. Strawn was born near Holcomb, Mississippi on August 30, 1925. At 18 years old, he volunteered to join the US Army Air Corp (now US Air Force) and served over 3 years in Germany overseeing reconstruction projects. He left active service as 2nd Lt, served several more years in reserves, and retired as Captain.

1. Q: What were you doing prior to joining the military?
    A: *I was growing up in a very poor time (The Great Depression). Prior to joining the military I had just finished high school and had been working for a couple of months at a mechanic shop until I was 18. Then I volunteered for the Air Corp. I did not have a sweetheart at the time but I was going out with other girls.*

2. Q: What do you remember about arriving in your first location?
    A: *Just the fact that this was something that I wanted to do. Both of my brothers were already in the military, one in the navy and one in the Air Corp.*

3. Q: How did you feel?
    A: *I actually did not have to go to war. I was the youngest male in my family and my two older brothers were fighting in the war. I could have stayed home but, I just felt like this was something I need to do.*

4. Q: What did you think of your commanding officers?
    A: *Very, very good. Training was so strict that you even had to eat a certain way. There was a thing call a "square meal" in which you ate, standing up, in almost robotic movements and your utensils had to be in a certain way. If we were to do anything wrong during our "square meal" we would have to give a "gig slip" to our commanding officer. If we gave too many we would have to march up and down the halls with our rifles on our shoulders for an hour or two. We did this to learn discipline and I believe this is something that most kids these days need to learn.*

5. Q: Can you please tell me about your two brothers?
    A: *Well my one of my brothers was 18 when I was 4 so all throughout WW II he was serving in the Pacific. He actually was fighting on islands that had Japanese soldiers still on it so he saw danger. After his tour in the Pacific, he continued to fight in the Korean War. My second brother was drafted before WW II began and was accepted into the Air Corp with only an 8th grade education. He was sent to England. During one of his missions, his plane was badly damaged and his crew had to ditch in the North Sea. After being rescued, his crew was given a brand new B-17 bomber. Shortly after its first take-off, the plane malfunctioned killing everyone on board. My brother and his crew have a memorial built in their honor at the site of the crash in Redlingfield, England.*

Links to Video of Interview and Poetry Reading:

http://www.youtube.com/watch?v=hmonVHnfnNc

http://www.youtube.com/watch?v=XIImR3jlWhQ

Aidan Danaher

For the interview, I had a conversation with my aunt, Joy, who taught me about Bulgaria and her life as a young child during WW2.

The first question I asked my aunt was how she witnessed the events that happened during World War 2. Her experience about the war was very unique to hear about because it was from the point of view of a very young child. Just as people comfort children during a storm, she was comforted and looked after in the same respect. "Because you're a little child, everyone was really nice to you," she said. Her memory during the war was that everybody was so kind to the children because they didn't want the children being scared, even though she said that it was scary for her.

The next question I asked was if she remembered her father, Luben Christov, who is my great grand father. The family was from Bulgaria, and my great grandfather was forced to fight for the Germans. She explains the very event that she remembered:

"My god, it was a Sunday and we were out in the country. And the car was stopped and there were soldiers with guns, and they took him. And he said that 'My family is in the car, I have 2 small children, I need to get them home. I promise I'll come back.' What they did was they followed us, he brought us home and then he went. At some point he ended up fighting them, what we would call today guerilla fighting."

She told me that she still hates guns for the reason that her Father had to fight a war, and even exclaimed that she can't bare war movies, and was never able to.

My next inquiry asked her about her experiences during the war, and she remembered a particular event on Christmas Eve, when the family had spent the night in a bomb shelter:

"We lived in Sofia, which is the capital, and Sofia was bombed. Constantly. The British bombed it during the day, and the Americans bombed it at night. . . We had a bomb cellar in the house and we had to go down in the shelter when they would have alarms. (There was) a Christmas Eve . . . and this alarm went off and we had to go down into the bomb shelter. And I grabbed this little tree that I had gotten, which was artificial, and I cut it up and fed it to my dog!"

One question I had to ask was if she remembered her family's feelings about the Nazi's and about the Communists.

"Well, yes I do. Especially Granny Lili's [my great grandmother's] feelings. She had basically no use for either one, but her frame of reference was that she personally didn't lose any family members to the Nazis, but she did to the Communists [meaning my other great, great grandfather]. In retrospective, the communists were really worse."

I asked her if she remembered the end of the war, and she answered simply:

"Do you mean like when they photographed people dancing in the streets in America? No I don't. What I remember is that the bombing stopped. People were happy it was over, but the place was such a wreck that nobody was happy. It was just destroyed."

Another question that I had asked my aunt was how the family dealt with rationing of very hard-to-come-by ingredients at the time, such as milk, butter and sugar. The answer was quite interesting:

"Stuff that we would consider staples was extremely hard (to come by.) If you were fortunate enough to have some money, which my family did, there were certain things you could get from what you refer to as the Black Market. Don't ask me where it came from, but some people had access to it, and if you knew somebody and you had the money to pay for it you could get it. I personally, have no memories of being deprived of stuff like that. We were not deprived at all."

One story that my aunt told me was that their house in Sofia, Bulgaria, was next to a small Catholic church, which was run by a Monsignor, who later became Pope John. During the war, he had cared for my aunt and had the nuns treat her for German measles. I thought that it was a very cool fact that he had helped her during this time of war and strife.

The final question I asked her was when she came to America after the war, after having her first Coca Cola, what did the Statue of Liberty mean for her? She answered, "All I thought was that she was beautiful."

Picture of Grandpa and his family

Wartime Picture of me (in the backyard

My Father, Grandfather, and Me

The Greatest Google Generation Interview

Interviewer: Andrew Meylan

Interviewee: Lenz Meylan (Grandfather)

Reason for Interviewing: Obviously, I have a personal connection because he is my grandfather. Secondly, I thought his story would be intriguing because until high school, he spoke German exclusively and was a first generation German-American.

Question 1: Do you remember the Japanese attack on Pearl Harbor.

> Answer: "December 7, 1941. I was at a play hosted by Loyola High School with my mother when I heard. I had to go home and look up where Pearl Harbor was. I had never heard of it."

Question 2: When war broke out, what aspects of your daily life changed?

> Answer: "We as civilians were most affected by the government rationing of everyday commodities like gasoline, shoes, meat, butter; we had to use food stamps and were only allowed 3 gallons of gasoline a week."

Question 3: Because of your German heritage, did you feel at all uncomfortable?

> Answer: "Until I went to school, I spoke German all the time, but when Hitler came to power, my parents decided that it wasn't a good idea to speak German anymore. I did not feel at all uncomfortable at school though."

Question 4: Do you remember either VE day or VJ day?

> Answer: "I remember VJ day most. I was coming home in my father's roadster going through downtown LA and everyone was going crazy and celebrating. For VE day everyone was still worried about getting deployed to the Pacific so no one was as relieved."

Question 5: What changed in your everyday life after the war ended?

> Answer: "Like I said earlier, the only thing that really changed was the government rationing. However, when the veterans came home, they all wanted new cars but it took a while to get the industry running again so they had to place bids and wait on a list."

*Student: Michael Breen
*Veteran Interviewed: Ned Breen
*Relationship to Student: Grandfather
*Date and Location of the Interview: April 21, 2012 in Griffith Park

I have decided to interview Ned Breen, my Grandfather, for many reasons. He was a very honorable and remarkable man. He has done many things that make him where he, and his family, is today. He has told me many stories from his past in World War II but now I want to know the specifics.

Q: Did you enlist or were you drafted?
Mr. Breen: "I enlisted on March 7, 1943. I was 18 years old. I didn't really have a choice of what branch I wanted to serve in, I was told to go into the Army. When I started out I was a Private. When I completed my role in the Army, I was a Corporal. I started out at Fort McCollum in Alabama and was there for 17 weeks doing ROTC Training. From there I went to Camp Howes in Gainesville Texas. Then I went to Newport News, Norfolk to be shipped overseas to Italy where I served most of my time.

Q: What do you remember about your first days in the military?
Mr. Breen: "A lot of marching, drills, talks and seminars on different subjects, a lot of classes on how to care and clean our equipment. Night problems were very excessive taught drills especially when I was in Georgia because it was too hot in the daytime. Night problems are what we called it when they gave us a compass and put us out in the middle of nowhere and we had to find our way back."

Q: What was your everyday like?
Mr. Breen: "When we were on the front lines they gave us K-Rations which included 4 biscuits that we called dog biscuits, 4 cigarettes, a small pouch of coffee and a small can of bacon with egg and cheese mixed. We also got C-Rations which were a mix of hash, beans, and stew in a can. D- Rations were also given to us, we got three pieces, and it was chocolate candy. I wrote many letters home. I missed my family more than anything and they meant the world to me. I wrote to my loving sister almost every time I got the chance. I was eager to get home. The conditions were and are very hard to picture. We had to smell the dead for many days then pick them up and mass bury them, dig through their stuff so they could be ID them. Their own uniforms would rot off their body before they could get another one. If they were so, death was sometimes wished upon instead of living the hell they were in. We were not able to shower for days, sometimes even weeks. We all smelled the same so you could not tell who was worse off, but then sores begin to appear then you have plenty to be concerned with.

Q: What did you do to pass the time?
Mr. Breen "We only had one person come to entertain us when I was in Naples, Italy. I forget who it was though. To pass time, I would converse with the people around me and grow a solid relationship with them. One of my best friends is one that I fought alongside."

Q: What did you do after the service?
Mr. Breen: "I was married. I had to come home and work and care for my family. It was really hard to find a job so for five months I did landscaping then I went to work in the Steel Mills. I went back to school in 1950 and took automobile repair under the G.I. Bill while I worked in the mill."

the food, something happened that seemed to destroy our expectations for a joyful holiday celebration. A member of the Dutch underground approached us. They had an urgent request that we shelter a Jewish family, a mother and 2 sons, This family had been hiding on a houseboat in our town, it was immediately necessary that they change locations since the German Gestapo was searching for them. Since protecting Jews under the Hitler regime, was considered a crime, punishable by death for the entire family we were faced with making a very difficult decision. Should we follow the dictates of our hearts, which said yes, or the dictates of our minds, which said no? We asked ourselves if as parents of 3 young children were acting in a responsible manner if we took this family in. We also knew if we did not shelter them, it would mean their death. We prayed earnestly that that family would find another place to hide. Then we waited to see what would happen. At 6 o'clock in the evening, there was a knock on the door. It was the representative of the underground informing us that they had not been able to find a hiding place for the family. Would we take them in? My wife and I looked at each other, then said bring them here! I never awaited guests with less enthusiasm! At 7pm on December 24, our hunted guests arrived. They carried a small bundle of clothes and a few scraps of food, which the underground had provided. The electricity had been cut off for some time and there was no heat. We did have a few stumps of candles, which we were saving for Christmas. So after drinking a cup of substitute tea, we all went to bed. It was Christmas day the next morning. I went next door to our neighbors, a Roman Catholic family, to wish them a merry Christmas. Just as I went out of the door, my wife suggested that I invite the neighbors to our home to celebrate Christmas together. We had to introduce our guests as our relatives from another town, and say they had lost their home with a bombardment by German planes. Since this was a common occurrence, it would not be questioned. Our Christmas celebration 1944 promised to be a very peculiar one. There was no Christmas atmosphere, as we had known in the past years. No multicolored lights, no gifts, no roast pheasant and other festive foods, no candles, no room filled with happy people who shared our faith. Our refreshments were a few slices of bread, substitute tea and 12 people of different faiths, brought together in very trying circumstances to celebrate together. After reading the first account of Christmas from the gospel of Luke, chapter 2 we started to sing the familiar Christmas songs, one after the other. In spite of the lack of all the material things usually associated with Christmas and in spite of the ever-present fear, we felt a blessing coming over us, such as we never experienced before. There we were, sitting on the couch together, two Roman Catholic neighborhood girls, our 2 two Protestant daughters and our two Jewish guests. They all sat together, singing "GLORY TO GOD IN THE HIGHEST" No, this was not an Ecumenical dream, it was reality. To my wife and I the heavens were opened that night and we all caught a small glimpse of that great Universal church. Now, many years later, we still feel that the Christmas of 1944 had been the strangest and yet most wonderful Christmas of all."

Student: Franco Ciccone
Civilian Interviewed: Cornelia Vande Beek
Relationship: A friend's grandmother
Date and Location: April 22nd- 24th, 2012/ via email

I chose to interview Cornelia Vande Beek because I had been hearing for years from my friend about how his grandmother lived in Holland during WWII. When I was assigned this project to interview a civilian or a veteran, it came to my mind that she would be perfect to interview. I was also intrigued to hear the story of a non-Jewish woman, because it seems to me that you mostly hear about the horrors that the Jewish families faced. I visited her in Santa Barbara and we talked a little bit about her history, and she agreed to let me interview her via email.

1. Do you remember exactly what you were doing when you heard the news of the war breaking out?

I was sleeping when the war broke out May 5, 1940, around 4am. I woke up due to sirens, screaming, German planes in the sky, and large German tanks entering our streets.

2. During all the years of the war, at what point do you remember being most afraid or worried?

I was most frightened when the Gestapo came looking for my father. He was hiding under the house (we did not have a basement), with several other young men. He had a small radio there and they were listening on the BBC to Winston Churchill. My mother cried, stating that my father was not here and she did not know where he was. I thought then, how strange, my mother would never think of lying!

3. In the heart of the war, how would you describe a normal day for you and your family?

We as children, up to the last year of the war were able to go to school. Monday, Tuesday, Wednesday, and Thursday were full days from 9-5. Friday and Saturday were half days, 9-12. When we returned home on Saturday, all the windows had to be washed and that was my job! My mother would be preparing food for Sunday. We all went to church twice on Sunday. All that routine changed the last year of the war. Schools were closed. There were many bombings and shootings in the street. Two of our neighborhood boys were killed in front of our house. We all lost one year of education. It was a very difficult time for parents, not knowing if you would be alive or what you had to eat. We each had one piece of bread per day, which we would cut in 24 pieces, then eat it very slowly. Have you ever tried to do that?

4. Do you remember the day that Germany invaded Holland?

There were rumors of war for several weeks before the war started. I was only 8 and did not have any idea what that meant. My parents tried to keep a normal routine and did not show their anxiety or involve us as they made decisions.

5. What do you remember about D-Day?

D-day arrived, a happy time. Canadian forces liberated us and gave us cigarettes and chocolate bars. Many became ill after eating the chocolate. The Swedish planes came, bringing us bread and butter. We were dancing in the streets. The most wonderful part of the war was that all churches worshipped together in one location. Of course that changed after the war ended and everybody went his or her separate way.

6. Did you ever have confrontations with the Germans?

We were fortunate to live near a farm and were able to pick up milk each day. I had that job, going on my bike without tires and hiding the milk under my coat. The German's sometimes caught me; they let me go without the milk.

7. Is there any other exciting or important story you would like to share?

May 1940, I was 8 and 13 when the war ended in 1945. It was very early in the morning, and the sky was filled with German planes dropping bombs and tanks rolling down the streets. It was an anxious time for us all and many prayers were said so the Lord would keep us safe. All stores were closed and all money cancelled. My Dad was involved in the underground, in charge of our province and had to hide because he was under 45 years old. All males under that age had to report to the Germans, but many hid underground. We had a 3-story house with hiding places under ground and in the attic. From time to time we had many people hiding, relatives, friends and a Jewish mother with 2 boys. That family tried to escape to Switzerland but the father was caught and killed. Food became very scarce. We received some food coupons and the Germans gave us vegetable soup for lunch at the central kitchen. I received a meatball on Friday's because I was 13. The last winter of 1944 was very difficult, little food and we ate bark from the tree and dried Tulip bulbs. The doctors said that if the war had lasted any longer we would not have survived. We all were very skinny with big bellies. There were times you had to hide 2 German soldiers overnight and it is amazing no one was ever caught in our home. One of my uncles was caught, sent to Germany and was able to escape.

"Franco, there is one last thing I would like to share. It is an entry that my father wrote in his journal":
"It was almost Christmas, 1944. The dark winter days seemed to be darker than ever that year. This was especially true in our country, the Netherlands. The allied troops that had landed in Normandy a few months earlier with the purpose of liberating Western Europe from the Nazi terror had not yet reached the Netherlands. Although hope and faith in the final success of our allied army was still strong among the Dutch population, the immediate future looked very dark indeed. Shortly before Christmas, after having been pushed back by the Russians and in the West and by the Americans, the Germans surprised the world by launching a powerful counter attack from the Rhine strongholds, through Belgium to the west coast, thus cutting of the Netherlands from the allied troops in Belgium and France. All food supplies had been completely halted and the Dutch were near starvation. My family was more fortunate than many of the Dutch citizens, because we had a few good friends who were farmers and their farms were located about 60 miles from our home. I felt sure that these good people would share some of their homegrown produce with us, if they possibly could. So I went on my bike a week before Christmas and rode to the farms and succeeded to get some valuable food. Air-filled tires had long since disappeared and riding a bike with only the frame was exhausting. Nevertheless I was filled with good cheer. The food would make it possible for us to have some Christmas celebration with our children. I arrived home 2 days before Christmas, exhausted, but happy. My wife and I began right away to unpack the food, some wheat, bacon and a few eggs. We ground the wheat in a small grinder, making it possible for us to bake real bread. In spite of the gloom throughout the country and total absence of all the external festive signs that tell us that Christmas is coming, my wife and I were filled with happiness that we, with our children, would have a good Christmas. The same day I returned with

From left to right (Jackson K. Coleman, Nancy Culbertson (Dean Keil's second child), Dean Emerson Keil, Frederick Coleman, Margaret Coleman (Keil's third child), and Tyler Coleman (the youngest of four grandchildren).

You have an amazing father, whom I'm proud of to call my grandfather. I hope you enjoy the story.

Love you, Aunt Nancy

Jackson

flight (maybe 20 planes of six men in each plane) went out a mission and couldn't strike their target because of cloud cover and for a while they were touch-n-go, but he didn't talk much more about his missions and left out many details.

The Air Force's men were able to go back to camp and relax on days they did not have a mission; however, the food was "terrible" but as Keil says he was hungry and more than willing to eat as an 18 or 19 year old. Lt. Keil remembers the worse conditions as living in a tent city somewhere near France no more than a couple of months, but in other places, like Brussels his unit and he could go around town and ride a bike, or play cards, or even see a movie or USO show; however, the mission days were long and hard. On those days the whole squad would spend hours briefing and debriefing, let alone in the plane, then after surviving another day of battle, the squad would enjoy a drink or two and rest. In Lt. Keil's down time, he wrote to his mother in Iowa, but he couldn't say much besides for hello and comfort her, because Keil's father was also working in the Hawai'i for the Navy.

Lt. Keil was somewhere in Belgium on V-E Day, but when news finally reached him and a brother in arms, they decided to drive through Germany in a Volkswagen and reached the Swiss border. The troops in Europe had sometime before they were sent state side. Keil was on a transport boat in New York City on V-J Day , but the troops on the boat were not allowed to leave the boat because they had to be discharged in California for some reason. But the end of the war "meant returning to normal life, and an end to excitement" for Lt. Keil. However after the war, Dean Keil's excitement would continue after he received his degree from Iowa in 1947, when he "left for an FBI job," where Mr. Keil would continue working until 1975. Since then, he's been a public accountant enjoying less hours, his family, and his silence.

He doesn't keep in contact with any of his comrades, but he didn't want to remember much about them. Although he never got too attached to his comrades and he gets a magazine from the American Legion every year, he could not want to try to remember those terrible events. The pain of the memories may be too much for him, so I told him I loved him, good night, and thanks for the interview. Even to his grandson, he just said "good bye, now", not cold- heartedly, but that's all he ever says, even though I know he loves me. But just like his story in the Air Force, he won't tell you anything unless you specifically ask him.

Jackson K. Coleman

Mr. Line

U.S. History, Period 1

27 April 2012

Lt. Keil

All my life I've known my grandfather and respected his past, courage, and honor because he lived through the Great Depression, but now, he shows little emotion. As long as I can remember he never boasted about when he was a lieutenant for the Air Force or government man, but I recall myself repeating that noise like a broken record. Because I haven't understood the full depth of the Second World War, nor will I ever know. My mother says he can't even watch a war movie and would sometimes wake up with night terrors and sweats. My grandfather's story begins when he was a little older than I am today.

As an 18 year old farm boy from Marengo, Iowa Dean Emerson Keil knew only of farms and the University of Iowa; however, in his sophomore year, he remembers his saddened mother on 7th of December 1941. Keil vaguely remembers his mother learning of the attack on Pearl Harbor where his older brother, Carrol Dean, was stationed. But thankfully, a couple days later his family received word that Carrol had survived the attack from the Japanese. The strike on Pearl Harbor affected his motive to enlist, but he knew he would either have to enlist or he would be drafted. Dean describes his feelings towards the branches as, "everyone at my age knew that we would be in the military, but I wanted to fly planes," but Keil would need to go to boot camp in west Texas first.

In west Texas, Keil was never truly scared about boot camp, and the training was "not hard, but so completely different to that [he] had experienced before." Keil also depicts the confusion of boot camp because he was "a farm boy put into a situation with all these kids of 18 or 19 into a staging area" (where men were determined if they could fight for America) learning how to march in formation and carry a rifle. Finally after basic training, Keil continued on to advanced training where he learned how to fly different planes in Fort Stockhom.

After he became a pilot, he flew a B- 26 from Florida to Ireland with his six man unit, which consisted of his co-pilot, bombardier, and three gunners. As the war continued his unit moved from Ireland to London, but mostly in Paris, then in Brussels. Keil flew a total of 36 missions over Germany bombing "bridges, railroads, and [enemy] staging areas." Lt. Keil flew strictly bombers both the B-26 and the A- 26, because bombers are not too mobile fighter planes would escort the bombers to the targets. However, he quickly stated being surrounded by dog fights "frequently" with some sense of confidence that he had seen them regularly on missions. Nonetheless, Lt. Keil earned several medals; standing out from the others is his Purple Heart. He earned the Purple Heart when his plane was taking enemy fire damaging the instruments, but he states he "was not injured badly" modestly as if they gave out Purple Hearts to soldiers with scratches. Another mission which feared Lt. Keil the most was one time when his

Jarrid Cooper
Nancy Willis
Family Friend
23 April 2012 Nancy's House

My interview was on Lorenzo L. Willis. Lorenzo died unfortunately, so his wife, Nancy Willis, answered the questions on his behalf. I chose to interview Nancy because she is a family friend and I always love talking to her. Nancy acts like she's in her 20's. She has the lingo and attitude of somebody my age, which is 15, so I always get a kick when we talk, especially about her youth. When I say she has the lingo of somebody my age I mean that she knows all of our slang words that most of our parents have no clue of including some like: leggo, meaning let's go or come on, only used in elevated times, filled with adrenaline, but a certain dialect is needed to say it; swagger, meaning a person's coolness, mainly being suave; YOLO, meaning you only live once; function, meaning party; etc.

The Interview

1. **Where was Lorenzo living before he joined the military?**
   He lived in Shreveport, Louisiana.
2. **Do you remember where Lorenzo attended high school?**
   Yes, he went to Parker High School in Birmingham, Alabama.
3. **Were you his sweetheart before he joined the military?**
   No, his first wife, Erma Lee, was his sweetheart. I was his second wife.
4. **Was Lorenzo drafted or did he enlist?**
   He was drafted.
5. **Do you remember what branch of the military he joined?**
   Yes, he joined the Army and became a Staff Sargent.
6. **Do you remember anything he told you about his first days in the Army? Whether it is his days in boot camp, his feelings, his instructors, or any advanced training.**
   All I remember him saying was that he did his boot camp in Savannah, Georgia. But he did do some advanced training I believe, if his unit, Anti-Aircraft Unit, counts.
7. **Where was Lorenzo first stationed?**
   He was stationed over in Africa in a place called Algiers, Algeria. He would always tell me that most of the Algerians looked like Blacks or Native Americans from Louisiana. He said that he would walk up to somebody thinking that they were from his hometown when really they were actually just Algerian.
8. **Was he ever stationed anywhere else?**
   When he left Algiers, he came back to America but he went to Wyoming.
9. **What was he doing during the war?**
   He was in the supply unit of Anti-Aircraft. He was in charge of sending things out to the battlefield.
10. **Did he have any close friends that he kept in touch with after the war?**
    Yes, he had one really close friend. His friend was wounded in Algiers but when he was discharged he moved to New York City.
11. **Do you remember what he did in his past time?**
    He went to USO shows in Savannah, Georgia.
12. **Did he ever come home on leave?**
    Yes, he came back home, I don't remember why but I do know he did take pictures with brothers.
13. **When was Lorenzo discharged?**
    He was discharged in May of 1945.
14. **After the war, did he go to school and take advantage of the GI Bill?**
    Yes he did. He went to school for construction. He was in construction for quite a while but then he started selling cars at a Volkswagen dealership.
15. **Where was he living?**
    After the war, he moved to Los Angeles to go to school for his construction.

http://www.youtube.com/watch?v=0s2xuRT6zRo

Student: Jesse Martinez
Veteran/Civilian: Teresa Redhead
Relationship to Student: Grandma of friend
Date and location of the interview: Graham Good's house; 4/24/2012

I chose to interview my friend's grandma because I found it interesting to get the perspective of someone living in England at the time of the war. Rather than interview a civilian living in the United States who would probably have the same mindset as a fellow American, I thought it would best to get a different point of view. It was a great choice for I felt I couldn't have heard some things that were told to me from just anyone else.

Q: Where did you live at the time of World War 2? How old were you when the war broke out?
A: I lived in the city of Lancaster which is in Lancashire which is in the north west coast across from Ireland. I was 5 years old when the war broke out.

Q: What was everyday life like? How was it like after?
A: For me it wasn't too bad we lived in an area that wasn't bombed but we heard the sirens because they [planes] would fly over to bomb Barrow-in-Furnes which was across the bay from us and we would go downstairs and get under the stairs or table. I would never go to the air rig shelters my mother would never let me go to the air rig shelters. But, we never actually got bombed, we would get scared when we would heard the German planes. When we were little in school we would taught how to put on gas masks they had little one for babies called mickey mouse's. That's the only time I remember being afraid because we would only be scared at night. After the war food was still rationed, it was like we were still in the war when it came to food.

Q: What do you think was your most memorable experience? When you realized something bigger going on?
A: Actually when the war ended, it was a marvelous experience, we were getting prepared for it and we had spare land and we built great big bonfires when and stayed out all night it was fun! By that time I was 11. It seemed like all night to us.

Q: Do you remember how you felt about Germany at the time?
A: Well we were kids so we sorta hated the Germans because they were the enemy. That was the general feeling towards them. I have since met German people over the years that I like very much but as a child well we all hated the Germans.

Q: Do you know anyone that was involved in the war? How did you feel?
My neighbors, my father worked for a big petroleum company and he was 35 when the war started so because of his age and because of his job he wasn't drafted in the military but he spent quite a bit of time away from home during the war in places that were getting bombed more and was supplying planes with fuel. I had an uncle who did not come back who died in Japan actually in Jarvis, a prisoner of war to the Japanese. We never knew- we were never informed of what happened and then finally one man came to talk to my aunt and told her he was with him when he died, he died of dysentery. I didn't like the Japanese because of what happened to my uncle, even when I first came to this country I had this feeling towards Japanese people but I learned to like everybody doesn't matter what the color is or religion or anything and I acccpt people as I find them.

They were satisfactory, you lived in the barracks with other guys and you had your own spot. You had a footlocker to hold your belongings. We had 20-30 people in the barracks.

Was there time when you felt stressed or homesick?

I think everyone was homesick. We were kids 18-19 years old.

Did you believe in any "good luck charms" or superstitions?

No, I did not believe in that sort of thing.

Did you come home on leave?

No, no, not from over sees. But when I finished cadet training I got to go home for a week or two and I did go home.

http://www.youtube.com/watch?v=rH1KPZWdDAc
http://www.youtube.com/watch?v=NtHsIRBjs14
http://www.youtube.com/watch?v=MKf8Eob_ERs

Student: Andrew Mackel
Veteran/Civilian Interviewed: Bill Main
Relationship to student: None
Date and Location of Interview: 04/24/12 Camarillo World War 2 Museum

Since I had no family that fought during World War II I had to search. I called my grandparent and other relatives to see if they knew any but they did not. I was able to find two veterans at the Camarillo World War 2 Air Museum. I went out to the museum located in the Camarillo Air Port and interviewed them both. They both had a lot of interesting and different experiences. They are now involved in restoring World War II planes. The questions below were the answers of Bill Main.

Did you enlisted or were you drafted?
I enlisted. Well I was born and raised on an Iowa farm and I didn't care much for that dairy work. It was obvious that I was going to be drafted so I took a chance and enlisted and some how I got through the whole program. I enlisted in the Air Force.
Did any of your friends enlist?
Well I was from a small high school in Iowa and I think we had about 42 graduates. Most of the guy waited to be drafted. But there were a few that were enlisted. I couldn't tell you the exact percent. The guy that enlisted had enlisted other categories like the army or air force. As far as I know I was the only one who enlisted in the Air Force.
What did you envision it would be like after you joined?
Well, in my case you had a standard program of training as cadet and so forth. But by the time you got out of the Castle Air Force Base there. You got a choice whether you wanted to be a fighter pilot or an air transporter. I chose to be air transporter. A lot of the more daring people went for fighter planes.
Where did you go during the war?
My combat was out of England, Eight Air Force. We bombed Germany.
Did you travel to other places?
We stayed mostly on one base. It was called Bury St Edmunds in New England. We all did different jobs and for some reason I don't think they like me. I had to fly B-17's from France to England that had been shot down and repaired just enough to fly back to England. Then they finally put us at a place called Stone England and we sat around there for quite awhile. I then flew a Warburg B-17 and brought it back to the states. I flew 35 missions with no had to hand combat.
Where you awarded any metals or citations?
I got about 6 air metals for the number of missions flown and I keep them in the office.
What was everyday life like?
Well a lot of it was just boring. The weather was not the most exciting. It was, of course rainy, foggy, or in climate weather in England.
Did you write letters? Did people write letters to you? What did you want to say?
O yeah you kept in contact with your folks and so. They had what they called V mail then. The sizes of the letters were decreased to save cargo room. They were of course censored quite a bit and the best part about it was it was free.
What was the food like? Did you always have enough food?
We did, it wasn't really the greatest but it was plenty, as food is concerned.
How were the other supplies and equipment?
The supplies were good and the medical care too. One time I had some dental work done and it was great.
What were the living conditions like?

The Greatest Google Generation
Student: Nick Pombar
Veteran/Civilian Interviewed: Mr. Denison speaking on behalf of his father, James Denison
Relationship to the student: Counselor's father
Date and Location of Interview: April 24, 2012 in Mr. Denison's office

World War II began with Germany's Hitler invading Poland in 1939. Britain and France declared war on Germany after Hitler had refused to abort his invasion of Poland. The United States entered the war when Japan launched their surprise attack on Pearl Harbor. It was then their business to get involved. James Denison fought for the United States in this war.

Q. What was your father doing before he joined the military?
A. Before being drafted, he was an attorney in the late 20's. He went to Yale and then Michigan. After that, he became an attorney in Los Angeles for the federal government.

Q. Where did you go during the war?
A. He spent most of his time in France and a little bit of Germany.

Q. Do you know how he felt about Japan or the war in Europe prior to Pearl Harbor?
A. He believed that it was a justified war, and that Hitler needed to be stopped.

Q. How were his first days in the military?
A. He went though boot camp, got tested, and eventually made a radio repair man.

Q. Was he awarded any medals or citations?
A. He was awarded the Silver Star for Bravery.

Q. What was his everyday like?
A. His everyday was pretty mundane. He did drills, wrote letters, maintained positions, and spent time with his comrades.

Q. What was it like after the war?
A. He went back to LA and bought a home. He had a sense of wanting to start a new life.

combat in Tunisia.   He talked about how he would see people hiding in Italy in caves from Mussolini and talked a lot about that and how ridiculous it was.

Q: What Do You Remember About The Other People in Your Unit?

A: Alvin Jackson was his close friends and he had many other friends; He kept in touch with Alvin Jackson up until Alvin passed away. He thought very highly of his officers and was very good friends with Mr. Jackson. He never spoke of casualties although he was bombed quite heavily by opposing German and Italian forces.

Q: Were You Awarded Any Medals or Citations?

A: My great grandfather was awarded the European African Middle Eastern Ribbon and the Good Conduct Medal. He earned from his years of Service over time. He really did not show off and brag about his medals. He just wore them on his uniform. He was a very solemn person and kept to himself quite often. He really did not like to talk about the war very much, but when he was asked to talk about it he did.

Q: What was Your Everyday Life Like?

A: He wrote letters home to his wife, and to his mother as well as his sisters. His mother, his wife, and his sisters all wrote back to him. They lived in tents on the battlefield so the living conditions were average. He was very homesick and stressed at times because he did not really want to fight in the war. He had religious medals from home that he brought over and pictures of his loved ones that he brought. He always said he wasn't ever in a situation where he didn't have what he needed supplies wise.

My Grandparents and I on my 12th Birthday. My grandfather is the one on the right

Current Photo of Me

Student: Mekai Sheffie

Veteran/Civilian Interviewed: Willard Robert Sheffie
(Interviewed Willard Robert Sheffie Jr.)

Relationship to Student: Great Grandfather (Interviewed
Grandfather)

Date and Location of Interview: 4-23-12, Phone Interview

Q: What Were You Doing Before You Joined the Military?

A: My great grandfather started and lived most of his life in Assumption Parish, Louisiana in
Bell Alliance Area. He attended St Augustine school for his grade school and part of high school
until he was homeschooled by his grandmother and his mother. He only had three years of
organized school, so he was in and out of being homeschooled. He worked as a farmer before he
went to the war. His sweetheart was my grandmother Thelma Lambert, who he eventually
married before he went off to the war.

Q: Did You Enlist Or Were You Drafted?

A: My great grandfather was drafted into the war. He did not choose his branch of service. He
was enlisted in the Army Air Core. He really didn't want to go to war but he saw the need to
help his country and it was the law so he did what he had to do.

Q: What Do You Remember About Your First Days in The Military?

A: My grandfather recalls that my great grandfather had a friend Alvin Jackson, who would
watch at program on T.V. called "Victory at Sea". He talked about how he was very nervous
and scared for the war. He said when he was bombed by the German machine guns he would
always get his rosary and start praying to God. War was hard and taxing for him.

Q: Where Did You Go During The War?

A: He was first station in Alabama. Neither the city nor the base was listed on his military
record. He lived in military housing with his wife on the base until he went overseas. He spent 1
month 1 year and 28 days doing service in the United States. He then went on to spend 2 years 1
month and 5 days overseas fighting the good fight. He had four military tours while overseas.
The places he fought in included Tunisia, Sicily, Naples, and Rome.

Q: What Were You Doing During the War?

A: His main specialty as listed was being a duty solider, which meant that he did whatever he
was ordered to do. He was a machine gunner at first, and then he was transferred to a
headquarters platoon where he became a cook. In the first year when he went overseas he saw

Timmy Mehl
Hans Mehl
Grandpa
4/26/12, Manhattan Beach

5. He was stationed in the Hitler youth. At the age of thirteen he joined this group. He lived throughout Germany for two years, until the war ended. The Hitler youth was comparable to the Boy Scouts today, however, it was much more intense and taught the doctrine of Hitler's beliefs.

6. During the war he also worked as a baker's assistant. This was in a small town named Whithoven, Germany, which was in South Germany.

9. Food was very scarce and they ate mostly potatoes and things including potato bread and things of that nature. Meat, sugar, and fresh fruit were very hard to come by. Most clothing items were made at home including pants, shirts, and jackets. Shoes were also very scarce. The house they he lived in had no air conditioning or heating. The winters were very cold and kept warm by a wood-burning stove. It was a very stressful time because his father was fighting for the German army at the Russian front.

10. To pass the time him and his friends, in his small town where he grew up, were building a BMW motorcycle from pieces that they have found, stolen, bought, and begged for. They spent many nights in his garage with his friends building their BMW motorcycle.

13. After the war, everyone came together to help rebuild Germany. Major cities had the most damage. They would travel once a week to Munich and Augsburg to help with the rebuilding effort. They would collect and remove debris or help rebuild houses by doing ruff carpentry or brick and mortar work. That process continued for many years until he decided to leave Germany and come to the U.S in 1956. He arrived in New York where his new life began as the head Baker.

Josh Woodward
Mr. Line
World History II, Period 4
26 April 2012

Google Generations Project

I chose to interview my neighbor Paul Horner. I've known him my entire life and never knew that he had any amazing stories or facts to share. Thankfully my mom talked to him about it and he said he would love to do an interview. I chose to interview him because I had heard that he had interesting stories to tell and can still remember the events pretty clearly. He was a kid during World War II in England which had a big impact during the war. Many kids in England during the time were separated from their parents and had to be evacuated. He was a very lucky child that was not evacuated from his mom while his father was in the RAF. After the interview I found it very interesting and am truly amazed at the chaos that transpired during World War II and would love to study and learn more about it.

1) How old were you during the time of WWII?
     Born in 1939, in January, the war started in September, born just before the start.

2) What was your everyday life like?
     Lucky, family evacuated. born in Stockton-On-Tees...Teisdal was the area. Evacuated to Middle-On-Teesdale, very remote country village. Country side, green, People in London, built air-raid shelters. In London they would sleep in the subway. Wasn't shipped away from parents like most kids in England. Lived in a miners cottage, was built in the 1800s, Middle-On-Teesdale was known for slate-mining. My family would bring out a tin tub and would use boiled water that was boiled in a kettle for baths. The toilet was out in the yard. In the night they would have to use a chamber pot. Everyone was issued with a gas mask. My mom couldn't put the mask on me, luckily they did not drop mustard gas. My family lived on the edge of the forest, there was a prisoner of war camp there.

3)Was there ever a time when you/your family were scared?
     Only 1 time there were bombs dropping. In the middle of the night, while my father was in West Africa. Mom was really terrified, a plane was dropping bombs in the fells, a part of the country side, a German guy dropped bombs there because he knew no one was there and he was tired of the war.

4) What was the food like? Did you always have enough?
     4 ounces of butter per person per month, 1 egg per person per week. We would make an omelet with one egg for 3 people. They gave us ration coupons. Everything was short, never saw a banana until I was 7. Farms where I lived, would give my "cute" mom extra eggs. Sometimes we did run out of certain things and ate whatever there was. We grew our own food, planted our own seeds. One day they said candy would stopped being rationed, lines of people for ever single item rationed. The next week candy was back on the rations.

5) Were any direct family members fighting in the war?
     My dad was commissioned in the RAF, he was stationed in West Africa. My dad was barely young enough to join the war, my father was 41-42 when he was called up. He never discussed what happened in West Africa, didn't talk about how life was.

6) What did you do for fun?
     Movies...movies were a lot of fun. I can remember seeing Carmen Miranda a Latin-American actress that would wear huge platform shoes and had very big hair. Really enjoyed the big time hollywood movies, a breath of fresh hope. Hollywood played a huge role to uplift the people who were struggling. I went to kids matinees at the Cozy Cinema, the only movie house where I lived. One time during a movie the usher was looking for me, the usher brought me my first ever ice cream. It had suddenly become available.

7) What did you think of American soldiers?
     Yankee soldiers were so glamourous, "you got any gum chum?" was something that we used to say to them because they always had chewing gum. Americans always had money to spend and candy that they would give out. We loved the yanks.

 Paul Horner as a teenager in 1950.

Student: Aaron Jaramillo
Veteran Interviewed: Buck Sargent Rudolph Delgato Curiel
Relationship to the student: Great Uncle
Date and Location of the interview: April 24, 2012 Via Skype

Q: What where you doing before the war?

A: I was working in an electrical plant. I worked for the biggest lumber yard in Los Angeles. I was married, I lived in east LA. I started Los Angeles City College in September of '39 but i dropped out because I got married. I was drafted in october and spent 38 months in the US Army.

Q: What do you Remember about your first days in the military? Do you Remeber anything from boot camp.

A: What an experience, first they shave your hair and then they give you everything in the world to carry up a great big hill, too the top of fort ord and you drop things along the way but you pick it up and you make it to the top. and thats just the beginning, than they ship you to be trained in camp Roberts in Paso Robles for 10 weeks. From there I did my ten weeks, then I was shipped off and told I was going to hawaii and ended up in south dakota at fort mead near an indian reservation for airborne we were going to be gliders and paratroopers. along with us were a lot of boys from east L.A, we were all drafted at the same time. a whole bunch of us, we had been in elementary junior high, high school and college and there we were meeting each other from different times. from there we were shipped around the country to the carolinas, to North Carolina South Carolina Georgia to different places, and we were shipped out in december of 45 we were sent to france we were there 9 months.

Q: What was your everyday life like

A: We were always in barracks or tents we were allowed to go home on furlough, I wrote home to my wife as often as I could, which wasn't everyday. The food wasn't like home cooked meals, they fed us whatever they felt like feeding us. In the winter we trained in the carolinas, and then we were shipped to france we arrived there in january.

Q: Do you remember when the war ended.

A: We were in france and we were suppose to be fighting along with general Paton, our job was to land behind the lines and take a city called worms. but he had already captured worms, so that mission was called off. then we had another jump to do. we were to go beat then to the rhine, and again Paton beat us there finally they sent us to denmark as occupation troops. so then I had free time and I was allowed to go to a university in paris, I was a good student in france. And then they called us back to go to japan, so they put us in a boat and a few days after at see they dropped the bomb and that was the end of the war. The Japanese surrendered and so for all of us we got to go home for good when we arrived in new york after that it was civilian life. I was discharged on December 22 after 38 months in the service.

Q: What was it like after the war?

A: The first 10 weeks your home they give you certain amount of money every week for about 10 weeks just to get used to civilian life, then after that you start looking for a job. I applied various places, and eventually ended up with a civil service job interviewing people at the los angeles hospital my job was to interview patience for medical need and financial ability to pay. And after a year I decided there was no future there and I wrote to The University of Southern California and in 2 years I completed 84 units of college credits and graduated and put in another year of training and began 30 years of working with Los Angeles city schools and retired in 1982.

Youtube Video link: http://www.youtube.com/watch?v=aiuesrsj0qw

The P-51 Mustang Fighter Jet that the Tuskegee Airmen flew Q: Where did he go during the war?

A: He and the other men were shipped out of Alabama to Northern Africa on April 16, 1943. The 99th Pursuit Squadron set up camp just outside of Casablanca, Morocco in the middle of a large dirt field. They were there for about 3 months waiting for their orders. Daddy spent most of his time their training the other crewmen and sightseeing.

Then they were reassigned to Tunis, Algeria. Clovis loved it there because he spoke French. This made it easy for him to get around the and mingle with the Algerians. The squadron was only there for a few weeks before they moved to Palermo, Sicily.

This is where the flight training really started. Pilots from the famous Flying Tigers of Burma came to Sicily to teach them how to be real airmen. The

Flying Tigers were a group of ex-military airmen who volunteered to fly fighter planes to defend the China against Japanese military invasions.

Most of the training was done in P-39 Airacobra and P-47 Thunderbolt fighter planes just like the ones that the Flying Tigers flew. These planes were old, heavy and very dangerous to fly if you did not know what you were doing. The crewmen and Lieutenant Benjamin O. Davis, or B. O. as his men called him, hated these planes. But they did not have any choice in the matter and the Flying Tigers trained them extremely well.

After they completed their flight training they shipped out to Naples, Italy. Clovis and his crewmen really enjoyed their brief stay in Naples. They loved the food and the people treated them really well. But after about 6 weeks they shipped out again. This time they were moved to a vacant field on the shores of Adriatic Sea. During this time, Clovis got to meet General George S. Patton when he visited Lieutenant Benjamin O. Davis.

After his visit the 99th Pursuit Squadron were given P-51 Mustang fighter planes to fly. These were much safer and more modern planes to fly but they had to be modified to fly long distances. So Clovis and his men were given the important assignment of adding gas tanks to the wings of the planes so that could attack places hundreds of miles away.

Once this job was finished they were reassigned to Rome, Italy. They did most of their missions from a secret airfield North of Rome. He stayed there until July 16, 1945.

Clovis (second from the left) and the other ground crewmen after arriving in Palermo, Sicily

Q: What was his everyday life like?

A: Clovis enjoyed his free time the most while he was in Sicily. While they were there they lived in villas just a few yards from the Mediterranean Sea. He always loved to swim so that's how he spent a lot of his free time there when he wasn't performing regular maintenance on the planes.

Clovis fell in love with living near the ocean while he was there. He probably ended up living in California because of how much he loved being in Sicily. He became a beachcomber there, just passing his time swimming and exploring the seashore.

Later when he went to Naples he got exposed to opera. There were a lot of opera houses where he went to see plays. He had heard opera music on the radio before he joined the Army. But seeing a live opera blew him away and he listened to it regularly for the rest of his life.

Clovis also got interested in photography while he was in the Army. He bought his first camera while he was in Naples and started to take pictures of places and people that he saw and met while he was in the Army. Photography became a lifelong hobby for him.

The food was horrible while he was in the military in the United States. While they were in Alabama, they were on a steady diet of stale bread, spam, and undercooked potatoes. And even on his free time he could not go to any of the better restaurants in Tuskegee because of racial discrimination. So even though they were American citizens their day-to-day lives improved when they were shipped overseas.

The food in Sicily and Italy were great. He said that he saw a lot of signs around Naples that had the word "Pizza" on it but he did know what it meant and did not find out until years later after he returned to the United States. The pasta and gelato were the two foods that he enjoyed the most while he was there.

In addition, the Italians were not racists like the American soldiers and citizens. They treated the African-American soldiers with honor and respect. They did not call them niggers and they hung out with them in bars, restaurants, and opera houses. The white soldiers never did so.

Their living conditions improved a lot when they went overseas too. While they had to live in tents for almost 6 months in Tuskegee, they were usually put up in villas or big houses when they were first assigned to Sicily and Italy. While they usually lived in the boondocks, outside of major cities near air fields, they always lived in safe, clean places overseas.

He wrote my mother often during that time. He also kept a picture of her in his helmet, even though he hated his helmet and tried to avoid wearing it whenever he could. The weather in most of the places where he was stationed was very hot and made it uncomfortable to wear a helmet. He was never close to combat so he thought that wearing a helmet was a waste of time anyway. However, Lieutenant Davis made them wear helmets anyway because of Army regulations.

Clovis said that he was the most homesick while he was in Alabama. Having to live in the middle of nowhere in a tent while being surrounded by the KKK and other racist whites was the worst time for him. The discrimination was very stressful because it made living a normal life impossible if you were Black.

Student: Parker Jackson-Cartwright Civilian Interviewed: Jacques Bordeaux Relationship to the student: Cousin Date and Location of the Interview: April 14 and 15, 2012 in Van Nuys, CA

Clovis Alonzo Bordeaux is the subject of my interview with his son, Jacques. He was born on September 23, 1917 in St Louis, MO. He received BS degrees in Physics and Mathematics from Lincoln University in June, 1939.

He postponed his graduate studies on April 4, 1941 when he enlisted in the United States Army Air Corps (USAAC) during World War II as one of the original members of 99th Pursuit Squadron, the Tuskegee Airmen. The Tuskegee Airmen were the first African-American fighter pilots in the United States military. Many African-American men at the time prayed for the opportunity to defend their country.

Military Poster from World War II showing a Tuskegee Airman

Clovis was no different. He jumped at the chance to enlist so that he could be a part of this historic military unit. At the time, Black men thought that fighting in the military was the best way to achieve full citizenship in the United States.

He became the squadron's Technical Sergeant in charge of aircraft maintenance and repair. He served under Lieutenant Benjamin O. Davis, the first African-American to become a General in the United States Air Force.

Clovis was a member of one of the most important and famous groups of African-American soldiers in the history of our country. That is why I wanted to do the interview about his life. In addition to all of his great accomplishments, I am proud of the fact that he was my great uncle on my father's side of the family.

I am also proud of the fact that I actually got to know him and spend time with him. Unfortunately, he passed away on March 12, 2011 at the age of 94. But our family has a great deal of information about him. My second cousin, Jacques, did the interview with me and brought a number of records and photos along with him. One of the documents that he brought with him was a tribute that he wrote about his father on his 90th birthday entitled *The Saga of Dave and Mary and Neecy Stories: The life and times of Clovis A. Bordeaux.*   He referred to it a lot during the interview.

Q: What was he doing before he joined the military?

A: Clovis was studying Engineering at the Milwaukee School of Engineering. At the time he was engaged to my mother, your great Aunt Bernice, who was attending Stowe Teachers' College in St. Louis. As soon as he got his certificate in Radio Engineering he tried to find work. Even though he had degrees in physics, mathematics, and engineering, he could not work at radio stations in St. Louis or Chicago because he was Black. Clovis did odd jobs during 1940 and 1941 trying to decide what to do next.

Clovis at the Milwaukee School of Engineering (second row on the left)

Q: Did he enlist or was he drafted?

A: While Clovis was searching for permanent work, he read an article in the Pittsburgh Courier about an elite 'Colored' Army Air Corps called the 99th Pursuit Squadron. The article mentioned that the squadron would be all Black from top to bottom and that Army was looking for ground crewmen, especially radiomen and maintenance engineers.

This was the first time that the media publicized the possibility that Black men could actually fight and see combat in the military, much less the Air Corps. Plus he thought that this was a perfect job opportunity where he could put his education to work. The next day he went to the Federal Building in downtown St. Louis and enlisted in the army for four years and volunteered for service in the 99th Pursuit Squadron. His official enlistment date was April 4, 1941.

His advanced engineering training and education were just the qualifications that the military was looking for. They sent him to Chanute Field in Chicago, Illinois along with about 100 other Black new enlisted men. All of them were college graduates in technical or scientific fields.

It wasn't long before he was training the other radiomen and engineers in the unit because at the time his education and experience as a physicist, a mathematician, and an engineer was considered to be 'high-tech', especially for a Black man. Clovis got promoted to Sergeant almost immediately by Lieutenant Benjamin O. Davis, the Squadron Commander, because of his skills as a radioman and an engineer.

Clovis and his wife, Bernice, just after he enlisted Q: What did he remember about his first days in the military?

A: The new Airmen, as they were called, boarded a train in Chicago and headed south on their way to Tuskegee, Alabama. It wasn't a big deal for most of the men in his unit because they came from schools in the deep South like Morehouse, Hampton, and the Tuskegee Institute. They were used to the segregation and discrimination that Black folks had to deal with
at the time. "Colored Only" signs and the Ku Klux Klan were normal parts of their lives coming up in the South.

But Daddy was not accustomed to this kind of open racism and mistreatment growing up in St. Louis and being educated for a time in Milwaukee. He talked about how his whole experience with racism changed once the train he was on reached Memphis, Tennessee and all of the Black people onboard were forced to sit in a segregated 'Colored' car directly behind the train's dirty, smoky engine all the way to Alabama. He said that when the train arrived in Montgomery, Alabama he felt like "we had left the United States and now we were in a foreign country. ALA- DAMN-BAMA."

When they arrived he and the other recruits were lined up at the gate to the airfield. A white officer came out and welcomed them by asking their white Army Recruiter, "Capt'n, why did you bring all these niggahs down heah?" They were refused entry to the base, forced to get back on the train and taken to the Tuskegee Station because Blacks recruits were not allowed to train with the white recruits in Montgomery.

When they arrived at the Tuskegee Air station they were still in the process of building the barracks and the mess hall. The base was really a giant open field with a fence around it and one small building in the middle where a few white officers and civilians lived and worked. There was literally no place for them to live on the base. The first night they were forced to sleep on the ground out in the open. The next day, tents were sent over from the Montgomery and lived there for about 6 months until the barracks were finished.

The white Army recruiters and officers treated the Black recruits like animals. Clovis thought that these men went out of their way to show disrespect and hatred for Blacks during Basic Training. Even though all of them had advanced college degrees and advanced job skills, the whites frequently called them stupid niggers or flying monkeys and criticized their work unfairly. In addition, Black recruits were often punished for very small
infractions like having untied shoes or dusty uniforms. White recruits were never punished or even questioned about such small issues.

Steven Petrides
Mr. Line
Period, 4
World History

An Interview With Steve Lolonis

My grandfather, Steve Lolonis, was a 12-year-old boy living in a village in Greece during World War II. As a survivor of World War II, he qualifies for being a member of the "greatest generation." As I have grown up, he has been there every step of the way and has become a major role model and special person in my life. For these reasons, I picked him as the subject of my interview. He has mentioned stories of World War II in the past to me. However, during this interview I took the opportunity to truly understand the hardships he went through during the War, and the victory he felt when it was over. Hardships that I may truly never fully understand but have now learned about through this interview.

Q. Where were you living and how was life before the war?

A. Steve went on to say he lived in a small village in Greece about two hours outside of Athens. He lived on a farm and was the oldest of 5 siblings. Even before WWII, he lived a much harder life than I do now. Working on a farm, he explained, is a lot more difficult than any part of my life.

Q. Do you remember when the war first started?

A. "Yes," he said. He explained how at first the Italians under Mussolini tried to invade Greece. In his words, "Greece pushed them out to Albania and drove them in the opposite direction from Greece." Then by 1941, almost a year after the Italians initially attacked, The German Nazis who were allies with the Italians invaded Greece and nearly took over the whole country. In April of 1941, they entered his town and began to occupy it. "I remember it was around Easter, they came in with trucks and tanks and guns and everything else," he said he then added, "At first they did not bother us, and we did not bother them, we were cautious around them because we knew who they were, but we were not scared."

Q. What was the saddest/most difficult event or turning point for you?

A. "In July of 1944, they came through and burned my village," he said. Steve then added that it was in response to gorilla attacks on German soldiers. Steve recalled that the Germans came through during the day before 3:00 pm and burned all 180 houses in his village. The people of the village ran in fear and terror. His family took their farm animals, which were their "most valuable things" and ran up into the mountains. He alone, a 14 year old boy, ran into the valley because "it was on a dirt road that the German trucks could not catch me on," Steve stated. He returned to the village a few hours later when the sun was setting to find his grandpa and other old people shot and executed. Steve told me, "The elders did not run because they expected to be treated with respect." He then carried his grandfather up to his church, the only building left standing in the aftermath. He found his family a day later on top of a mountain with the rest of the village and with no food or shelter.

Q. What was every day like for you?

After Steve's village was burned his life was close to a nightmare. He lived through the rest of the War on top of a mountain over looking his village. The village was starving, with nothing to eat but "bread and tomatoes." Over 200 village members starved to death. Two of them were his cousins and many were friends from school. The whole town had one radio to share, in which they would listen to at night, and receive updates on the war. Steve's village would also receive letters dropped by United States airplanes. The letters would say that everything would be okay, and they would be "saved and taken care of after the war." Two specific events that he remembers were when he went to dig a grave and bury his grandfather, German's would drive patrol trucks and shoot randomly he remembers "hiding in fear when the trucks came driving by." He also remembers when the Germans were ready to move on to the next town. Greek "Gorilla Soldiers" ambushed them killing 47 German soldiers. Steve remembers watching from a distance and then said, "You're too young for me to tell you about all the blood and stuff that happened there."

Q. What was Life like After the War?

Life was so very exciting after the war had ended. Steve remembers in September of 1945 the Germans left. The day after, the American government sent ships as part of the Marshall Plan with "Everything, all sorts of stuff." They brought clothes, toys, food, medicine, supplies for houses and everything else they needed. Steve said, "It was one of the happiest moments of my life." The Americans especially liked his baby brother, Bill, for they gave him teddy bear after teddy bear. To this day Steve says, "All Greeks who lived through World War II love the United States and President Truman for all they did."

In the picture above, Steve, my grandfather is wearing a blue shirt and looking right at the camera. I am sitting to the left of him and two of his brother are to the right of him.

Student: Vincent Magcase
Veteran/ Civilian Interviewed: Ted Fujimoto
Relationship to the student: None
Date and location of the interview: 4/21/12 over the phone.

The reason I chose to interview Corporal Ted Fujimoto is because he had a significant amount of information about his time fighting in World War II. He has many interesting stories to share. Corporal Fujimoto is proud that he was able to be a part of this historical event that changed the course of life.

What were you doing before you joined the military?
I was born in North Central, California in a farming community a little south of Sacramento. We raised melons. At the time, Japanese couldn't purchase land so we had to share crop. Share cropping is when you share your profits with the person that owned the land. Before I was drafted I was a junior in high school. I didn't have a girlfriend at the time I was drafted into the war.

Did you enlist or were you drafted?
I was drafted in 1944 at the age of 16 and I served in the 442nd company of the U.S. Army.

Where did you go during the war?
I was sent from San Diego to Florida for training. After training, I was shipped overseas to Northern Italy for a rescue operation named the Lost Battalion. I remember one time where the Germans were on top of houses shooting down on us. We startled crawling on goat trails and would sometimes peek up to see where they were shooting from. Now that I look back on it, that wasn't such a good idea.

What was your everyday life like?
My everyday life was kind of boring while not in action. I wrote letters home to my two older sisters. My older sister's husband was part of the M.I.S. which is the military intelligence service. There was always plenty of food, but while I was in action we only relied on dry food, canned food, crackers, and cheese. I was never really homesick or stressed because both my parents had already passed away.

What do you remember about the other people in your unit?
The other people in my unit consisted of mostly Japanese Americans. We developed close friendships as time went on. I kept contact with a few after the war, but we no longer keep in contact because we live in all different parts of the U. S.

Corporal Ted Fujimoto (in red) taking a picture with other veterans from the 442nd company.

Student: Michael Padilla
Veteran Interviewed: Verl Lindley
Relationship to the Student: Aunt's friend
Date and location of the interview: Wednesday April 11, 2012. Quaker Gardens Senior Living, Stanton, CA.

Did you enlist or were you drafted?
I enlisted in the Air force because I preferred to be in the Air Force rather than be a man fighting in the trenches. I was originally assigned to put wire cable on the front line for radio communication, but that was not for me. Roosevelt canceled enlistments for the Air Force because there were not enough people that were joining the army. Then started my basic training to become a cadet. There was about 3 or 4 of my friends that enlisted at the same time but we all went on to different things.

What do you remember about your first days in the military?
The day we were inducted, they put us in an auditorium filled with about 500 guys. They came from two nearby high schools so most of the guys knew each other. People were joking around and the sergeant came in to introduce what was going to happen. I was sent to Arlington near Riverside and then sent to Texas for 3 months for the Army. But then I switched to the Air force.

What was your everyday like?
I wrote a lot of letters home, it was interesting to write the comments of what happened that day. There was always enough food; it was never a big problem. But, I recall that it was never any good. It was simple kinds of food and we always got meat. They gave us oatmeal and cereal in the morning. We had good equipment and had what we needed. We had fully equipped uniform and food. We lived in barracks, which was simple and plain. I felt homesick and stressed a lot. There were times where I felt alone.

Do you remember V-E Day and V-J Day when the war ended? Yes, I remember flying in Europe and it ended before the one in Japan. They brought us back to the states and we had just arrived in the Sacramento air base. We went to town that night and guys were grabbing girls on the street and kissing them. They sent me back east before I could be discharged.

Were you awarded any medals or citations?
Yes, one for being on the European theatre one leaf for every five missions, one for good conduct, one for missions flown, and one for shooting a rifle.

Video of the Interview: http://youtu.be/yck71ZVZLEA

Student: Luis Gaitan (son of interviewee)   Date of Interview 4/22/12
Veteran: Manuel Gaitan (uncle of interviewee)
Interviewee: Manuel Gaitan (nephew of veteran/father of student)

Sometimes when I'd sit down and watch TV with my dad, we'd talk about the show that was playing. Every now and again, there would be programs about World War II. "You have family that fought there," he'd tell me. There were several occasions where there would be a program about the death camps and my dad would turn to me and tell me, "Your uncle Manuel liberated some of those death camps." While watching a movie about Patton, he said to me, "your uncle was in an armored division with him in North Africa." When I put the pieces together in my mind, I thought: Wow! My great uncle was awesome! He seemed like an interesting character and I'd love to know more about him.

1. What did he do before the war?
A: My uncle worked for the gas company.

2. Was he drafted or did he enlist?
A: He enlisted into the US Army where he served as a Ranger and also served in Patton's 6th Armor Division.

3. Was he awarded any medals?
A: He earned a Purple Heart

4. Where did he go during the war?
A: My uncle went to North Africa. He served in Patton's 6th Armor Division. While in North Africa, his battalion walked into a German ambushed, where he was wounded. He recovered in time for D–Day. He landed on the beaches of Normandy on June 6th 1944. So much of his battalion was wiped out that he was sent back to Patton's armor division. My uncle was also sent to liberate the death camps in Europe. He caught tuberculosis (which he'd later on lose a lung to) while at the death camps and was later discharged.

5. What were some memorable experiences in the war?
A: One experience he had was when he walked into a building and the building exploded. All his clothes were blown off in the blast.

Others were his horrific experiences was when he was burring dead bodies at the death camps. He constantly saw people dying all around him. The medics had to tell the soldiers not to give prisoners the rations because the prisoners were so famished, that their bodies couldn't tolerate the regular food and would cause death. Since my uncle knew how to operate a bulldozer, he dug graves for the dead prisoners in these camps. This was a traumatic experience that haunted his memory banks until the day he died. He would be brought to tears every time he'd tell the story of liberating the prisoners of these harrowing camps.

Left: Manuel Gaitan (Veteran)

Right (from left to right): Manuel Gaitan (Nephew of Vet.), Luis Gaitan (Great Nephew of Vet.)

Student: Austin Adams

Veteran/ Civilian interviewed: Sergeant Leland Svarverud, U.S. Air Force

Relationship to student: Grandfather

Date and location of the interview: April 7, 2012 Roseburg, Oregon

When I was a young boy I would spend my summers in Oregon and every time I would visit my grandfather he we would tell me stories about the war and what he remembered most about those few extraordinary years in world history. Now that I am older and have a better appreciation and understanding of how great those stories were to our history I feel compelled to educate others on how important these times were.

Q: Where were you living before you joined the military?

A: I was living in Eugene Oregon

Q: Did you have a sweetheart?

A: Yes, In Salem but when I left for the war she sent me a "Dear John Letter" and that was the end of that.

Q: Were you able to meet famous war heroes of the time?

A: Yes, I got to meet Dwight D. Eisenhower after the Normandie Invasion.

Q: How did you get into the war?

A: I went to aircraft school and found a job in Los Angeles, California where I received my draft notice then I went back to Salem, Oregon. I was then sent to the Air core where I worked on B- 38 Bombers and also worked with the Civilian Conservation Core (CCC) on army and government projects.Q: Where were you stationed?

A: I was shipped to Laurinburg Maxton Army Air Base in North Carolina. On April 15, 1943 I was sent to Casa Blanca, North Africa. I was shipped out to Sicily in September of 1943 and then to England on Saint Patrick's Day 1944.

Q: What jobs did you have?

A: Crew chief and glider mechanic

Q: Can you tell me about your most memorable experiences?

A: My most memorable experience of the war was meeting my wife, Peggy Ball, in England and getting married on April 19, 1945 in England.

Q: Did you write many letters home?

A: I wrote as many as I possibly could.

Q: What were the living Conditions like?

A: The living conditions were not that bad at all. I had a dry bed and enough food so I couldn't complain much.

Q: Were there times when you felt homesick?

A: All the time, but once I got married and started to grow a family the feeling was less irritable.

Q: How do you still honor the memories of WWII?

A: I am part of a veterans association call the Warbirds in southern Oregon

Student: Fabio Bachemin

Veteran: Russell Stewart

April 24, 2012 at the Santa Anita Retirement Center where Russell now presides

I decided to interview Russell Stewart because of his high intellect on the subject along with his own experiences in a war. Even though he is not a veteran of WWII he is a proud veteran of the Korean War. His childhood and teenage years were effected by WWII.

Russell Stewart lived in Duarte, California, attended Whittier High school, went on to PCC, and played baseball before being drafted into the Korean War. Pearl Harbor occurred when he was around 11 years of age and as he said it changed his life. He can remember that day at the hour when he heard the news. Before the occurrence he did not think much about U.S. history, however, since then he became very interested. Because of this he has a clear view of who is bad and who is good during a war. He describes war as basically a battle between good and evil usually due to differing political views. Russell was drafted into the army in 1950 for the Korean War. He graduated from the CIC, Counter Intelligence Core, and was in top secret assignments. When in service the only thing he thought of was baseball and was never homesick due to his focus on what he was doing in the CIC. After leaving the army Russell went back into baseball. When he finished baseball, Russell finished college to receive his bachelor of science in business.

Jose Jimenez

I interviewed Mrs. Joan Carillo.

She is my aunt's Mother-in-law, this is how i know her.

I interviewed her on April 25, 2012 in her house.

I chose to interview Mrs. Joan because she was around during World War II. She had an uncle who was a soldier in the war. She remembers a few things about what went on around the time, even though she was young. She told me the few things she knew about her uncle.

Q1: From what you remember, what did your uncle do in the war?

A: I remember that he was in the Navy and that he was present on D-Day

Q2: Did he make it back home? or did he die when he was in action?

A: No, he died when he was away, but he sent us many letters telling us that he was okay, and asking us how we were. I had a serious cold and he also asked how i was doing in a letter. In one of the letters he said he sent us some money but we never got it. The government probably took it.

Q3: Do you remember how the people around you viewed the war?

A: I know that in the area where we lived, we really didnt like it because we didnt know what was going to happen, who was going to win or who was going to lose.

Q4: Were you worried at all during the war?

A: I was definitely worried, especially since I had a family member who was serving for our country. I didnt know how the future was looking for all of us, but we all stayed strong and confident that things would come out the way we wanted.

Q5: What was it like after the war?

A: There was definitely a lot of relief and happiness because the war was over and knowing that the US came up as a winner a lot of us had the confidence that no one can mess with us. But inside our family and other's families because of so many lives that were lost.

couldn't believe it could happen, so he stayed behind while the others went into their fox holes.

5. Question: What was it like after the war?

Answer: He remembers that his brother-in-law (who was in the war with him) was not able to find a job, so he enlisted in the army again and was killed. After the war, he lived in New Jersey and worked at the Brooklyn Navy Yard. He got a lot support from the GI Bill but could not take full advantage of it because some of his documents got washed away in a flood. He was the type of person who treated people the way he wanted to be treated, and he believes that this is one reason he was able to be so successful after the war.

Interview YouTube Link:
http://www.youtube.com/watch?v=6lHFicrxcd0

Student: Kelechi Nwachuku

Veteran/Civilian Interviewed: James King

Relationship to the student: Friend

1177 West Adams Street Los Angeles, CA, 90006/ April 22, 2012

       I met James King through a neighbor on my block. I'm first generation from Nigeria so I personally did not know any World War II veterans until I met James King. My neighbor gave me his phone number, and he happily agreed to do the interview. James King was, and still is a brave a man and I have the upmost respect for him for serving our country.

1. Question: What do you remember about your first days in the military?

Answer: He remembers getting acquainted with his surroundings/the military. He wasn't nervous. He told himself that it was something he had to do. His instructors weren't too harsh. They told him what he could and could not do and he had to abide by those rules. His instructors weren't openly racist but he could somewhat tell that they thought less of him because he was Black.

2. Question: Where did you go during the war?

Answer: He got his basic training at Camp Claiborne, Louisiana. He was first stationed at The European Theater of Operation. He stayed behind the line sending food, clothing, and ammunition to the front line. He remembers sending ammunition to the Tuskegee Airmen.

3. Question: What were you doing during the war?

Answer: He sent food, clothing, and ammunition to the front line and protected the buildings with these items in them (He did not see combat). When he was on the ship to Europe, he remembers a lot of the soldiers getting seasick although he didn't experience this.

4. Question: What was your everyday life like?

Answer: He wrote his wife every week. He missed her because he was in Europe for three years and only got married to her a year prior to him being drafted. He slept in tents and described the living conditions as good quality. He said that the Germans would wait until 3:00 in the morning to strafe their quarters. He was one of those guys who just

Student: Sean Leonard   **Veteran Interviewed:** Victor Hemphill Sr.

Date/ Location of the Interview: Phone Interview on Tuesday April 17th, 2012.

Intro: I chose to interview Mr. Hemphill after discovering one of his posts on a Veteran's Forum online. After sending an email off to him and, additionally, receiving a response, I wanted to pursue learning more about him.

Q/A:

Where were you living before you joined the military?
Lived in Times Beach Missouri, a town that no longer exists. The EPA bought the land up because of contamination and turned into a waste disposal site. Now a Route 66 state park. The town where I grew up and went to school no longer exists.

When did you enlist and what do you remember about your first days in the military?
I enlisted in the Coast Guard October 31, 1944 and went through boot camp at Government Island in Alameda, California.

What job assignments did you have during the war?
I was an officer who typed his way through the Coast Guard, typed the Smooth log. A ship's log is written by the officer of the day in long hand, and the permanent record is typed. I was responsible for typing the permanent record. When in New Orleans, I was transferred to Officer of the Commander of the 8th Coast Guard District on Canal Street in New Orleans dispersing department payment vouchers for men who were transferred.

Where did you go during the war?
After attending bootcamp for 90 days, I was assigned to troop transport ship General C.H. Muir AP 142 on the maiden voyage from San Francisco to Pearl Harbor. Then travelled to Antioch Island, then to Ulysses, and then to Mog Mog. Later, Lady Gulf in the Philippine Islands. Came back the same way through Pearl Harbor. Orders then changed to go through Panama Canal to go to New York and transferred from the Muir to General W.P. Richardson AP 118. Travelled to Strait to Gibraltar, Naples, Italy, Suez Canal, the Red Sea, Indian Ocean, India, and through the Persian Gulf and Iran.

Any Additional Notable Memories?
Remember the Japanese surrender, bombing of Hiroshima and Nagasaki. No memory at all of either ship. On VE Day of 1945, I was standing on the corner of Broadway and 42nd Street in New York City. Ticker tape lights on Times building announced the news.The place went wild, within minutes there must have been two million people in times square, it was INSTANT PANDEMONIUM.

Student: Ry Christiaansen

Civilian Interviewed: Freeman Bales

Relationship to the Student: Uncle

Date and location of Interview: April 13th, 2012, Freeman's house

I chose to interview my uncle Freeman because of his close relationship with my Grandpa, a World War II veteran. Grandpa Bud, who died in 2004, used to sit with my uncle and tell him about his experiences about fighting the Nazis in Europe.

What was Grandpa doing before he joined the military?

Grandpa Bud was living in Los Angeles, working at North American Aviation, building planes for WWII. He worked there alongside his future wife, who worked in the department of Weights and Measures.

Did he enlist or was he drafted?

Grandpa was drafted in Los Angeles in 1943 and joined the invasion of Sicily.

Where did Grandpa go during the war?

He completed his basic training in Texas then was shipped out to Palermo in Southern Italy. He then pushed north all the way to Trieste, Yugoslavia, essentially chasing the retreating Nazis.

What was Grandpa Bud doing during the war?

Grandpa was an extremely good typist, and worked right behind the front line, documenting events and communicating messages. He never saw combat, but remembered one of the scariest moments of his tour when the building he was working in was bombed during his stay in Sicily.

What was his everyday life like?

Grandpa had just married Grandma before he left and they were expecting a baby (me), so they wrote back and forth constantly throughout his tour. The food, supplies and housing were all excellent and abundant. Grandpa told me that he occasionally felt homesick, but always kept a picture of Grandma with him. He didn't really believe in good luck charms or superstitions.

Paul Schuck,

Paul Schuck, at the age of 20, resided in Ohio as a door to door donut boy. This was his job at the time, unfortunately during the Great Depression, until December 7, 1941. Paul had not heard of Pearl Harbor prior to this attack. He clearly remembers the day. "It was around 1 pm, they had announced on the radio that Pearl Harbor had been bombed." Paul was then drafted on Nov 23, 1942 and celebrated Thanksgiving in the army. Paul said, "I thought to myself, the army is going to be amazing if they server food like this everyday." Throughout his time served, he was awarded a few medals but his most prized is the Bronze Medal, a medal awarded to those with over and above actions in battle. Currently he belongs to the Disabled American Veterans Organization due to his hearing impediment.

What do you remember about the first days of the military?
Paul was initially assigned to the 81st Division. He had a 6 week training course prior to being shipped out. The training consisted of "field problems", obstacles and problems that a soldier will see in battle. At first, he was sent to the Pacific Theater; however, the army gave him a 10-day furlough. After the furlough, he was sent to the European Theater.

What did you do during battle? Where did you go during the war?
In October of 1944, Paul was deployed into battle in the European Theater. He was a "platoon runner," which was a messenger. His job was to communicate orders from the captain to the front lines. The communication was mainly through radio; however, if it failed he would have to run. Over his time served, he went to Belgium, Luxemburg, France, and Germany. He also crossed the Rhine River.

What was your everyday life like?
"I was fortunate enough to have been in a company." Companies would go over field problems in the morning for a few hours and then get critiqued on their performance. Then a 25 mile hike with all their equipment. However, on days when his company went into battle they would be on a lookout for days.

What was one of our most memorable moments?
Paul began, "It was the second week of April of 1945." Paul and his company discovered Camp Ohrdruf, "a satellite camp" of a larger camp. This camp had around 12,000 polish/Jewish refugees. This camp was a work camp not an extermination camp. After the capture, Paul noticed a lot of refugees were machined gunned down by the SSR because they knew Paul and his company were coming. The camp was about a mile from the city. Paul and his company went to the city and captured the house of a former SSR lieutenant. This house contained food and water in which Paul and his company distributed throughout the starving refugees.

Where were you when the war ended?
Paul was in Czechoslovakia. It was May 5, Paul was supposed to wake up at 3 am for a combat mission. However, he did not wake up until 8 am b/c "nobody had woken me up." "It was the best day of my life. Second was when they dropped the bomb on Japan. Third was the day I married my wife." The next day he was shipped out to Camp Kilmer where he showered and ate and then from there he was moved to Camp Atterbury. It was a separation center where he was then able to go home

was lucky, on the ship ride he was with a chef. The food the chef made was so good officers would sneak into their unit to grab some of it. He said he thought the boat ride was going to be worse than it actually was. Here is a picture of him going on the ship ride.

What was your everyday life like?
He said after I got to the small town outside of France they set me up as a typist. He has a great luxury of being in a second story building with a bed, he said it was very luxurious. He always would go and work out at a gym they found around a mile away. An officer then made him athletic captain, so he was in charge of all the sports. Here is a picture of him playing basketball. He went throughs his days and he said they started blending together. He shared with me two stories, the first one was about a German soldier and the other was about a hike with his officer. The German soldier and been shot by one of my grandfathers allies and when they went to search him the guy started to take his wedding ring, then my grandfather said "Leave the poor man alone, and even though we are on the same side ill have no problem hurting you if you don't let this man be, so you'll have to get through him to get to me." The other soldier left and the German soldier died in peace.

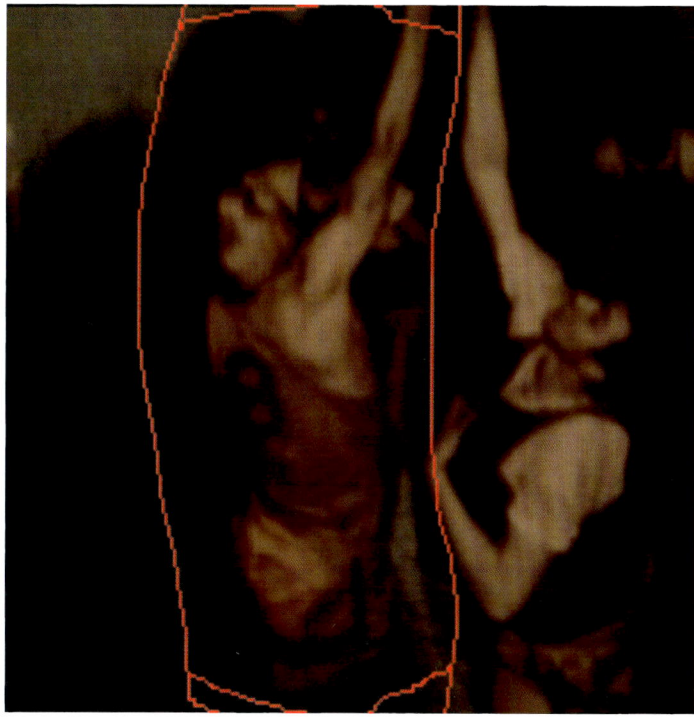

The second story was when my grandfather was going on a hike with his commanding officer, the the hike took two days and they had to sleep. So my grandfather accidentally slept in poison ivy and couldn't see because it got into his eyes. He asked the officer if he could come in the trailer they had, he said no and my my grandfather walk the last 15 miles on food unable to see. My grandfather did it with out any arguing. When he got back to his camp he said he was so sweaty and could't see so his comrades had to cut his clothes off and then they took him to the hospital where he was hospitalized for 5 weeks. This makes me proud and glad to call him my grandfather.

Youtube Interview:
http://www.youtube.com/watch?v=AHQT6aLjYgc&feature=youtube_gdata_player

Student: Connor Ellison
Veteran/Civilian Interviewed: Michael McParlane
Relationship to the student: Grandfather
Date and location of interview: 4/22/12 my house

Why did you choose to interview your veteran/
civilian: I interviewed my grandfather because he
was the closest member of my family that lived
through it and was part of it. My grandfather also
used to talk about it a lot, and had many
interesting stories. Now that I was older I was
able to appreciate the information this time.

What were you doing before you joined the
military?
He worked at a department store in Detroit,
Michigan, and he didn't have a sweet heart going
into the army. He was done with high school, he
was about to be twenty one years old.

Did you enlist or were you drafted?
He was drafted. He said all his friends got drafted but none were in the same unit or
area as him. He didn't really envision what it would be like joining the army, all he knew
was that he was called for his country and he
would go.

What do you remember about your first days
in the military?
He remembers how much of a change it was,
he said he was really no longer free. That
you always had to follow directions and had
some one bossing you around at all times.
He was excited to go though, he wanted to
serve his country he was a true american. I
then asked him on a scale from 1-10 how
hard was the first week and he said 8. He
then stated that his favorite part was boot
camp. I asked if any fights happened, he
started to laugh and with a giant smile said "I
wasn't part of and of that fighting." Here is a
picture from the day before he got drafted.

Where did you go during the war?
He said that he went to a small farm city outside of France. When he was being
transported from the States to France he was supposed to be going in a glider, but last
minute they put him on a different unit and he went on a cold boat ride. He said that he

very fond of him. In my mind, Dwight definitely fitted the criteria of what a military leader should meet in order to lead an army; he was the perfect man for the job.

Q: Did you ever aid or help out in any way during the war? (I.e. medical assistant, cook) And if so, what was your duty?

A: When I was a junior in high school, a few of my girlfriends and I went to work in a factory in Pennsylvania where we made hand grenades. I was in charge of putting the top part of the grenade together, which was during the final stages of actually constructing the grenade.

Q: What was life like after the war? And could you explain what it was like visiting Dwight in the White House or attending his Inaugural Ball in Washington D.C.? Finally, what sort of memorabilia do you have of Dwight's today that you cherish the most?

A: After the war was over, everyone was ecstatic because the fighting had ended and many men were able to return home to their families. Unfortunately, many families suffered financially because the U.S. was almost bankrupt after the war. Luckily my parents knew how to budget their money, so we did not suffer as much as others had.

Visiting Dwight in the White House was a once-in-a-lifetime opportunity that I was fortunate enough to take part in. I attended both of his Inaugurations as President, had several breakfasts with him in the White House, and even attended both of the Inaugural Balls with my husband, Lloyd. Today, one of my most cherished memorabilia I own of Dwight's is a photograph of him and all of his brothers together that [Dwight] actually signed and gave to me as a gift.

My Grandmother (Jean Greene) and Me
Spring 2011

Student: Peter Eisenhower Riemers

Civilian Interviewed: Jean Greene (Wife of Lloyd-Edgar Eisenhower; Dwight Eisenhower's nephew) (Dwight D. Eisenhower is my Great-Great Uncle)

Date and location of interview: April 18, 2012 (phone interview)

I chose to interview my grandmother because of her involvement in World War II and her direct ties to General and President, Dwight D. Eisenhower. My grandmother is a very significant person in my life with a lot of remarkable wartime stories to tell because she actually lived during those times and had a brother that served as a doctor in WWII and fought in the Korean War. Today my grandmother lives in San Francisco, and I see her periodically throughout the year around the holidays and for special family events.

Q: As a young girl, what do you remember about the war and what were your feelings about war?

A: I can vividly remember playing outside with my cousins on a Sunday afternoon and then coming inside my house to find my parents and aunt and uncle huddled around the radio. The adults tried to keep us children quiet because something important was being broadcasted over the radio, something that was life-changing. After the broadcast was over, my parents explained to my brother and me that the U.S. had gone to war with Germany.

Q: Where were you living during most of the war, and was the area influenced by the war?

A: As a young girl, I lived and grew up in Washington, Pennsylvania, which, back then, was a small city of about 2,500 people. All I can remember is that Washington was highly influenced by the war, and all of the boys in my high school class were enlisting for war, including all of the male teachers as well.

Q: Having relations to Dwight Eisenhower and his family, how did this affect your opinion about the war?

A: I felt as though Dwight was a very influential man (in a positive way), and spoke very confidently about his plans as a general in the war, which made people believe he knew what he was doing. Overall, though, I felt it was the right thing to do for the U.S. to go to war.

Q: Do you ever remember meeting Dwight and did you ever have a one-on-one conversation with him? What kind of person was he? In your mind, did he fit the criteria of what a military leader should have in order to lead an army?

A: Dwight was a very interesting man who was well educated military-wise. When I met him and had conversations with him, he was always polite and cordial towards me, which made me

EUROPEAN THEATRE

The European Theatre of World War II was a huge area of heavy fighting across Europe from Germany's invasion of Poland on September 1, 1939 until the end of the war with the German unconditional surrender on May 8, 1945 (V-E Day). The Allied forces fought the Axis powers in three sub-theatres: the Eastern Front, the Western Front, and the Mediterranean Theatre.

These are the stories from those who were there..